AEON FORCE

BOOK 1

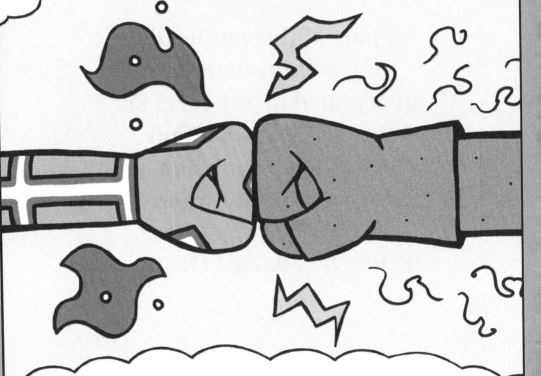

FOR THOSE WITH THE
COURAGE TO NEVER GIVE UP.

ISBN: 978-0-9763418-7-1

Book 1:
First Edition

HOW TO READ THE COMIC

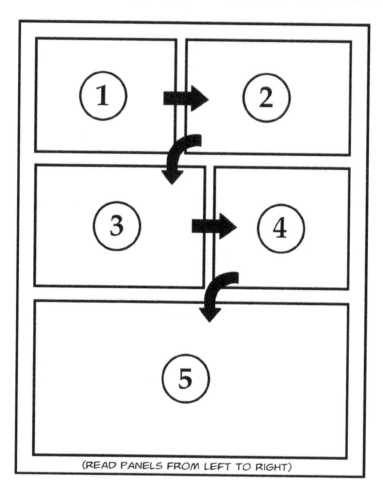

(READ PANELS FROM LEFT TO RIGHT)

CRMBLE!

CRMBLE!

CONTENTS

HAHA!

YUCATAN PENINSULA,
PLANET EARTH.
5133 BC.

ALRIGHT, LET'S TAKE IT FROM THE TOP! LONG AGO, IN AN ALMOST MAGICAL LAND, THE SEEDS OF CIVILIZATION FOUGHT HARD TO TAKE ROOT. IN AN ANCIENT WORLD SHROUDED IN ENIGMATIC WONDER...

CHAPTER 1: BURNT-PAST, BRIGHT FUTURE

I'VE NEVER BEEN THE BEST AT STARTING STORIES, BUT I THOUGHT A TRIP DOWN MEMORY LANE MIGHT GET THE BALL ROLLING. THERE ARE PROBABLY BETTER PATHS I COULD HAVE TAKEN WITH ALL OF THIS, BUT FOR ME, THIS WAS THE ONE THAT JUST FELT RIGHT.

AND IN AN ERA OF GREAT TURMOIL, A RAG-TAG GROUP OF WARRIORS AND SOME OUTCASTS FROM ANOTHER WORLD, JOINED FORCES TO... GAH! I'M NO GOOD AT THIS. YOU GET IT ALREADY. THIS IS A FLASHBACK.

7

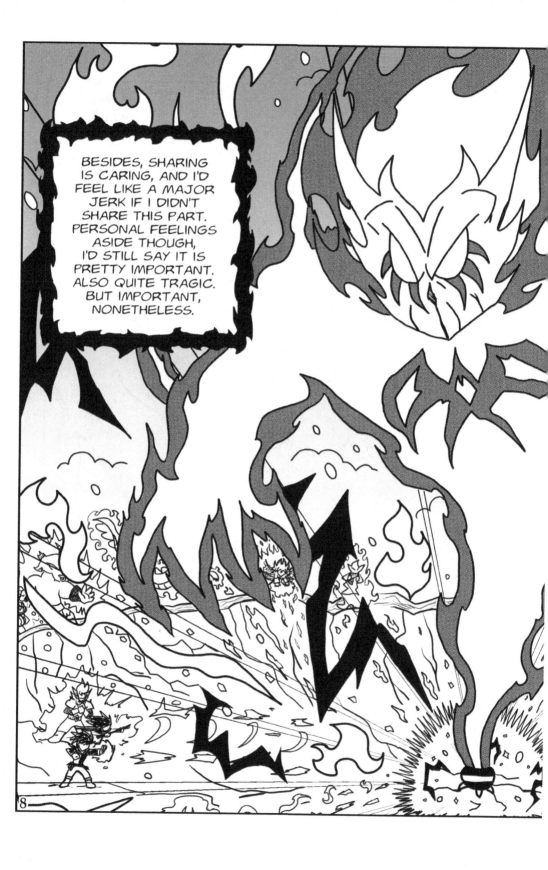

BESIDES, SHARING IS CARING, AND I'D FEEL LIKE A MAJOR JERK IF I DIDN'T SHARE THIS PART. PERSONAL FEELINGS ASIDE THOUGH, I'D STILL SAY IT IS PRETTY IMPORTANT. ALSO QUITE TRAGIC. BUT IMPORTANT, NONETHELESS.

HEY RUBY! BE A DEAR AND PUT UP SOME COVER FOR US, WOULD YA?

R-RIGHT!

BY THE POWER OF WORDS THAT SHAPE OUR REALITY!!!

AND STRIKE BACK TEN-FOLD!!

ENDURE THIS ATTACK...

MAX COUNTER SPELL...

KZKRRR!!!

KRKRR!!!

MIRROR FORCE!!!

GRAGHH?!

CRYSTAL PHALANX

THERE. THAT SHOULD BUY US SOME TIME.

NOW HURRY UP AND GET OVER HERE. IT'S TIME TO FINISH THIS!

GREAT WORK, RU!

BUT LADY MIRA, WE'RE GIVING IT OUR ALL TO COMPLETE THE SEAL AND...

IT'S STILL NOT ENOUGH!

HEHE! YEAH, MAYBE. BUT WE CAN'T COUNT OURSELVES OUT YET! I HAVE A PLAN.

WE'RE GONNA USE UP ALL OF THIS WORLD'S AURUM SUPPLY FOR ONE FINAL PUSH.

WE'LL COMBINE IT WITH OUR FULL POWER AND LOCK HIM AWAY FOREVER!

B-BUT LADY MIRA, IF WE GO THROUGH WITH THIS...

AND USE *EVERYTHING* WE HAVE TO COMPLETE THE SEAL... THEN THAT MEANS YOU AND EVERYONE ELSE ARE GOING TO-

DON'T WORRY ABOUT US!

WE CAME TO YOUR WORLD KNOWING FULL WELL THAT THIS COULD HAPPEN! WE'RE PREPARED FOR THE CONSEQUENCES.

12

BESIDES, WE WERE THE ONES WHO BROUGHT THIS MESS TO YOU. WE SHOULD BE THE ONES TO MAKE THE SACRIFICE.

W-WAIT! PLEASE, THERE HAS TO BE A WAY THAT DOESN'T INVOLVE LOSING YOU ALL! THIS CAN'T BE OUR ONLY OPTION!

FOR NOW... I'M AFRAID IT IS, RU. AS FAR AS OPTIONS GO, THIS IS ALL WE HAVE LEFT.

LISTEN UP, KID. OUR TIME LEFT TOGETHER IS SHORT, SO I NEED TO TELL YOU SOMETHING WHILE I STILL CAN. YOU'VE MADE ME PROUD. AND NOT JUST THAT. YOU'VE MADE ME EXCITED TOO. BOTH, TIME AND TIME AGAIN.

I'M PROUD OF ALL THAT YOU'VE ALREADY ACCOMPLISHED, AND I'M BEYOND EXCITED OVER WHAT YOU'RE GONNA DO NEXT. I'M NO GOOD AT LYING. I'M TOO BLUNT FOR THAT. SO EVERYTHING I SAY HERE'S THE WHOLE-HEARTED TRUTH.

MY GREATEST WISH IS TO SECURE THE FUTURE!

OR AT LEAST THE BEST ONE THAT I CAN GIVE TO YOU.

I'VE NEVER ONCE NEEDED A REASON TO DO WHAT I DO...

BUT NICE GOIN' KID! 'CAUSE MY FIRST REASON'S YOU.

15

16

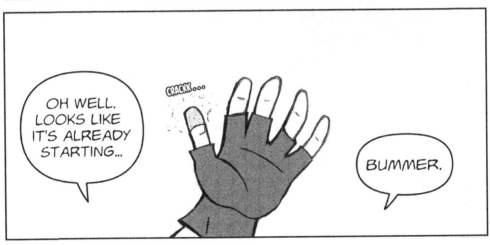

L-LADY MIRA?

HEY! NICE SAVE, THERE.

I... I'M SORRY, I DIDN'T THINK IT WOULD START SO SOON.

I CAN SHARE MY ENERGY WITH YOU TO SLOW IT DOWN. I'LL DO ANYTHING TO GIVE YOU MORE TIME!

NO... IT'S FINE, RU. I'D RATHER JUST TALK FOR A BIT, IF THAT'S ALRIGHT WITH YOU.

I REALLY LOVE THIS STONE YOU GAVE ME... BUT I SHOULD GIVE IT BACK TO YOU BEFORE I GO.

IT'S BEAUTIFUL. SO IT'D BE A SHAME TO LET IT END UP IN THE SAME PLACE I'M GOING. PUT IT SOMEWHERE YOU THINK IT'LL LOOK NICE, OKAY?

B-BUT MIRA, I-

NO "BUTS"!!

GOSH, RU. EVEN FOR WHAT MIGHT BE MY FINAL WISH, YOU STILL FIND IT HARD TO COMPROMISE. IT'S OKAY THOUGH. THAT'S WHAT I LIKE ABOUT YA, KID.

ALWAYS STAY THAT WAY. FIGHT FOR WHAT'S RIGHT, SAY "NO" TO THE IMPOSSIBLE, AND THE FUTURE WILL BELONG TO YOU. YOU'RE GONNA GO FAR... I JUST KNOW IT.

KRRR....

CRRR....

19

PRETTY SAD, RIGHT? YEAH. I THOUGHT SO TOO.
IT'S NOT FUN TO THINK ABOUT, BUT HEY,
WHETHER IT'S IN THE FORM OF SACRIFICED
TIME, EXCRUCIATING EFFORTS, OR THROUGH AN EVENT
THAT ALTERS THE VERY FABRIC OF YOUR PLANET AND
CAUSES YOUR BEST FRIEND TO TURN INTO A ROCK,
VICTORY NEVER COMES WITHOUT A PRICE.
IT SUCKS, BUT I DIGRESS.

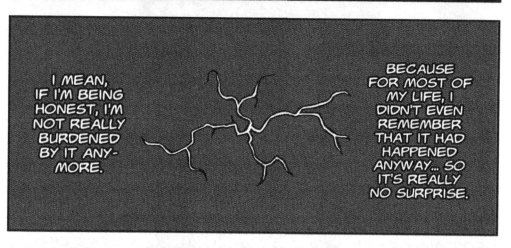

I MEAN,
IF I'M BEING
HONEST, I'M
NOT REALLY
BURDENED
BY IT ANY-
MORE.

BECAUSE
FOR MOST OF
MY LIFE, I
DIDN'T EVEN
REMEMBER
THAT IT HAD
HAPPENED
ANYWAY... SO
IT'S REALLY
NO SURPRISE.

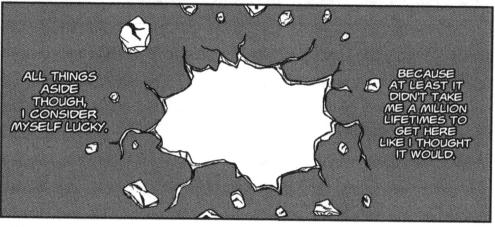

ALL THINGS
ASIDE
THOUGH,
I CONSIDER
MYSELF LUCKY.

BECAUSE
AT LEAST IT
DIDN'T TAKE
ME A MILLION
LIFETIMES TO
GET HERE
LIKE I THOUGHT
IT WOULD.

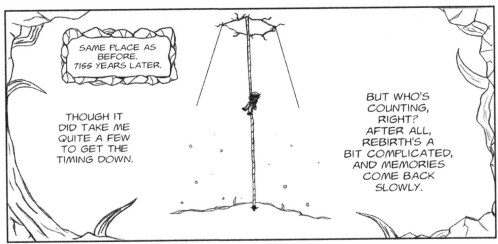

SAME PLACE AS BEFORE. 7155 YEARS LATER.

THOUGH IT DID TAKE ME QUITE A FEW TO GET THE TIMING DOWN.

BUT WHO'S COUNTING, RIGHT? AFTER ALL, REBIRTH'S A BIT COMPLICATED, AND MEMORIES COME BACK SLOWLY.

AT THIS POINT IN TIME, I DIDN'T REMEMBER MY PAST AT ALL ACTUALLY. BUT LUCKY FOR YOU, AS THE NARRATOR, TIME IS IRRELEVANT FOR ME.

I HAVE ALL THE WISDOM OF MY FUTURE SELF AND CAN EXPLOIT THAT FOR THE SAKE OF THE STORY. DON'T WORRY, THOUGH. NO SPOILERS.

BUT WHILE WE'RE ON THE SUBJECT OF WISDOM, ONE THING I'VE LEARNED ABOUT THIS WORLD, AND MAYBE EVEN ABOUT LIFE IN GENERAL, I GUESS...

IS THAT NO MATTER HOW MUCH TIME PASSES, NO MATTER HOW MANY THINGS CHANGE, AND NO MATTER HOW FAR YOU GO...

SOONER OR LATER, YOU ALWAYS END UP RIGHT BACK WHERE YOU STARTED.

CHAPTER 1, END. BOOK 1, BEGIN!

ADVENTURER'S NOTES #1

THE PLACE WHERE IT ALL BEGAN.

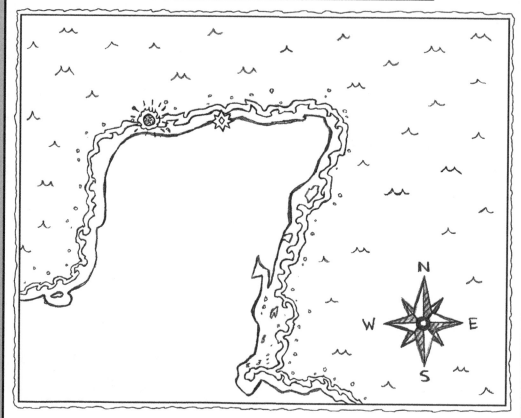

"WHEN ONE ADVENTURE COMES TO AN END, ANOTHER WILL BE BORN."

AEON FORCE

CHAPTER 2: THE SPIRIT OF ADVENTURE

CHAPTER 2:
THE SPIRIT OF
ADVENTURE

CHCK...

EXPEDITION LOG.
SITE 622:
TOLLAN FOREST.
DATE:
OCTOBER 12TH,
2022.

bzzt

WHAT IS UP
ADVENTURERS?!
AFTER BESTING A
SERIES OF ANCIENT
BOOBY TRAPS AND
OUTSMARTING SOME
DUNGEON PUZZLES,
WE'VE FINALLY
MADE IT!

APPARENTLY,
THESE RUINS
HAVEN'T BEEN
EXPLORED FOR
OVER 7,000 YEARS.
SO CONGRATS
EVERYBODY, WE'RE
MAKIN' HISTORY!

TODAY'S EPISODE IS
ALREADY OFF TO
AN EXCITING START,
BUT WE'RE NOT
DONE JUST YET!
THIS PLACE HAS
SO MUCH LEFT TO
SEE, AND THERE'S
NO TIME TO WAIT!
'CAUSE ALWAYS
REMEMBER,
ADVENTURE WAITS
FOR NO ONE!!

DRRIP

DRRIP

HAHA, BESIDES!

A GREAT ADVENTURER CAN ALWAYS SPOT A BLUFF, EVEN FROM A MILLION MILES AWAY!

SHHHHH

28

CRMBLE!!

JUST LIKE I THOUGHT... THESE BOULDERS ARE MADE ENTIRELY OF LIMESTONE.

CRMBLE!!

IN OTHER WORDS, JUST A ROCK MADE UP OF A FRIENDLY LITTLE MINERAL CALLED CALCITE.

ON THE MOHS HARDNESS SCALE, CALCITE HAS A PRETTY LOW SCORE OF ABOUT A 3.

SO WHEN MET WITH HARDENED STEEL, WHICH OUTRANKS IT WITH A SCORE OF ABOUT AN 8, IT ALMOST FEELS LIKE YOU'RE SMASHING THROUGH GLASS.

FUN FACT. LIMESTONE IS ACTUALLY ONE OF THE THREE MAIN INGREDIENTS GLASS IS MADE FROM. GO FIGURE.

PING!!
PING!!

THE OTHER TWO ARE SODA ASH AND SILICA. FEEL FREE TO IMPRESS YOUR FRIENDS WITH THAT ONE, THE NEXT TIME YOU WANNA SOUND SMART!

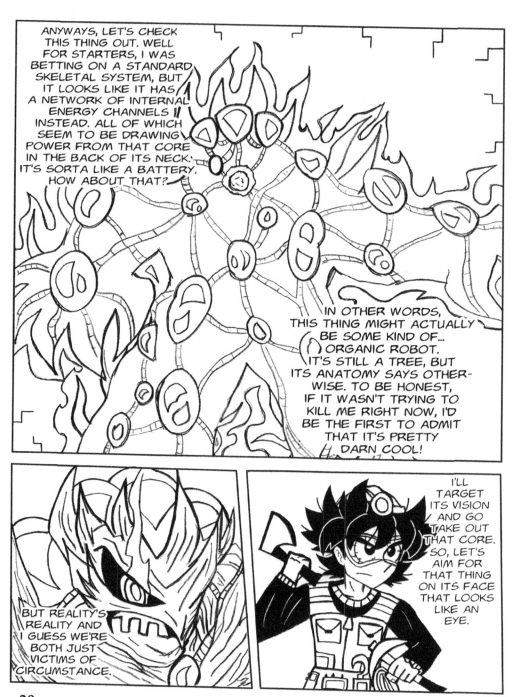

ANYWAYS, LET'S CHECK THIS THING OUT. WELL FOR STARTERS, I WAS BETTING ON A STANDARD SKELETAL SYSTEM, BUT IT LOOKS LIKE IT HAS A NETWORK OF INTERNAL ENERGY CHANNELS INSTEAD. ALL OF WHICH SEEM TO BE DRAWING POWER FROM THAT CORE IN THE BACK OF ITS NECK. IT'S SORTA LIKE A BATTERY. HOW ABOUT THAT?

IN OTHER WORDS, THIS THING MIGHT ACTUALLY BE SOME KIND OF... ORGANIC ROBOT. IT'S STILL A TREE, BUT ITS ANATOMY SAYS OTHER- WISE. TO BE HONEST, IF IT WASN'T TRYING TO KILL ME RIGHT NOW, I'D BE THE FIRST TO ADMIT THAT IT'S PRETTY DARN COOL!

BUT REALITY'S REALITY AND I GUESS WE'RE BOTH JUST VICTIMS OF CIRCUMSTANCE.

I'LL TARGET ITS VISION AND GO TAKE OUT THAT CORE. SO, LET'S AIM FOR THAT THING ON ITS FACE THAT LOOKS LIKE AN EYE.

30

WELL, IT LOOKS LIKE EYESIGHT'S OFF THE TABLE. THAT MEANS THE MOST LIKELY WAYS IT GETS AROUND ARE THROUGH SONAR, LIGHT OR THERMAL DETECTION, OR BY SENSING NEARBY VIBRATIONS.

LUCKY FOR US, WE CAN MAKE SOMETHING THAT ACCOUNTS FOR ALL OF THOSE THINGS...

JUST... DON'T TRY THIS AT HOME, PLEASE.

FIRST, WE'LL TAKE 3 PARTS IRON OXIDE AND 1 PART ALUMINUM POWDER. MAKE SURE THOSE PROPORTIONS ARE RIGHT OR ELSE YOU'LL MESS THIS UP! FOR OUR PURPOSES, WE'RE GONNA LAY OUT OUR INGREDIENTS ON SOMETHING FLAMMABLE, LIKE THIS MEDIUM-SIZED PIECE OF CLOTH FOR INSTANCE...

NEXT, MIX THOSE POWDERS TOGETHER, THEN GO GRAB A MAGNESIUM RIBBON. JUST MAKE SURE IT'S LONG ENOUGH. THIS LITTLE GUY'S GONNA SERVE AS OUR FUSE, SO BE A BIT GENEROUS, OKAY?

THEN, TIE EVERYTHING TOGETHER WITH A RUBBER BAND...

AND WE'VE GOT OUR LITTLE BUDDY THAT'S GONNA HELP US OUT BIG TIME!

NOW, ALL WE DO IS LIGHT THE MAGNESIUM FUSE ON FIRE...

AND PRAY THAT WE DIDN'T UNDERESTIMATE OUR RIBBON SIZE FROM EARLIER.

33

THOUGH IT IS A DISTRACTION WITH A VERY SET TIME LIMIT. SO I DON'T HAVE EVEN A SECOND TO WASTE.

WOOSH!

FRRRR!!

CRCK!

CRCK!!

CRSHH!!

SHHHHH

SHHHHH

34

35

WELP...

THAT'S ALL FOLKS!

AT LEAST WE DIDN'T DIE, SO I'M REAL HAPPY ABOUT THAT...

IT COULD'VE GONE A LOT WORSE, SO I DEFINITELY CAN'T COMPLAIN.

BESIDES, THAT TREE-BOT WAS SO COOL, I WONDER IF I COULD MAKE ANOTHER ONE WITH THIS!

AH... BUT THAT'S AN EXPERIMENT I'LL SAVE FOR ANOTHER DAY.

FRRRR

BESIDES, I KNOW A CERTAIN SOMEONE WHO'LL GO CRAZY WHEN THEY TAKE A LOOK AT THAT THING!

BUT FIRST THING'S FIRST, I'VE GOTTA GET OUT OF HERE IN ONE PIECE.

HOP

SMOOTH SAILING SO FAR...

BUT I DOUBT THAT'S GONNA LAST.

CLICK!

CHK!! CHK!!

TREASURE HUNTING RULE NO. 1:
IN ADDITION TO BOOBY TRAPS
BEING PLACED ON THE WAY TO
ANY SORT OF VALUABLE TREASURES,
THERE ARE ALWAYS EVEN MORE
TO WATCH OUT FOR ON THE WAY
LEADING *FROM* THEM, AS WELL.

BUT IF I'M BEING HONEST...

I DON'T REALLY MIND IT.

YOU SEE, I LIKE TO THINK OF IT AS A LITTLE GAME...

PLAYED BETWEEN ME AND THE OLD TRAP DESIGNERS.

THE COOL THING ABOUT IT IS
THAT IT'S ONE YOU CAN EASILY DO
WELL IN JUST BY BEING PREPARED.
IT'S NOT A GAME THAT TAKES ANY
TALENT OR BRAINS TO BE GOOD
AT. JUST SIMPLE WILLINGNESS TO
THINK AHEAD AND BRING THE
RIGHT TOOLS IS ALL THAT
YOU NEED TO WIN.

BOOM BOOM

BOOM

BOOM

BOOM

HOWEVER...

NOT EVERYONE APPRECIATES THE VALUE GOOD FORESIGHT BRINGS TO THE TABLE. SOME EVEN CLAIM THAT THINKING AHEAD IS JUST A SIGN OF AN OVER-ACTIVE IMAGINATION.

BUT THOSE WHO ARE DUMB ENOUGH TO BELIEVE THAT NEVER LAST VERY LONG...

SO WHO THE HECK CARES WHAT THEY HAVE TO SAY.

42

FWOOOSH

SKRRRT!!!

AND ONE MORE TIP...

THERE'S NEVER ANY SHAME IN BEING A SCAVENGER. SOMETIMES, THE BEST TREASURES ARE SIMPLY THE OLD AND DUSTY THINGS THAT SOMEBODY ELSE LEFT BEHIND.

BUT ON ANOTHER NOTE... IT'S TIME TO DELIVER THE BOSS SOME GOOD NEWS.

YOU'RE GONNA LOSE YOUR MIND WHEN YOU HEAR ABOUT WHAT I JUST DID.

YO DAVE!

OHO, REALLY? IS THAT SO, ALEX?

WELL, I'LL HAVE YOU KNOW THAT WHAT I'VE BEEN UP TO'S WORTH LOSING YOUR MIND OVER AS WELL...

GREAT! I GOT THE AUDIO FOR TOMORROW'S EPISODE, SO I'M WAY AHEAD OF WHERE I THOUGHT I'D BE.

REALLY?

NAH, NOT REALLY. I'VE JUST BEEN DECODING THESE GLYPHS IS ALL. IT'S ACTUALLY KINDA BORING TO BE HONEST. BUT THAT'S ENOUGH ABOUT ABOUT ME. HOW'D IT GO?

I ALSO FOUND THE HIDDEN BASE-MENT TO THIS PLACE AND DEFEATED A GIANT TREE ROBOT.

I TOOK FROM IT WHAT I THINK MIGHT BE SOME KIND OF ORGANIC BATTERY. BUT WHAT DO YOU THINK?

MY GOODNESS LAD! I-I-I DON'T KNOW WHAT TO SAY! MOSTLY 'CAUSE I DON'T REALLY KNOW WHAT THAT IS!

BUT IF YOU'RE RIGHT, YOU COULD TOTALLY MAKE ANOTHER TREE-BOT WITH THIS! THAT'D BE SICK!

YEAH, THAT'S WHAT I WAS THINKING! THOUGH THAT'S SOMETHING THAT I MIGHT TRY OUT LATER. THERE'S SOMETHING ELSE STILL DOWN THERE THAT YOU SHOULD CHECK OUT LATER TOO. IT HAS A *REALLY* STRONG AURA TO IT THAT I THINK YOU'D WANNA SEE.

REALLY?!

WELL, THEN FORGET ABOUT LATER!

UH?

BUT...

LET'S GO NOW!!!

BUT!
BUT!
BUT!
BUT!
BUT!

HUFF!

HUFF!

GAH! BUT I ALREADY WENT THAT WAY!

SIGH... WELL, WHILE HE'S DISTRACTED, I MIGHT AS WELL TAKE THE TIME TO FORMALLY INTRODUCE MYSELF.

MY NAME IS ALEX RUBINO. AND SO FAR IN THIS LIFE, I'M AN UNCONVENTIONAL 23 YEAR-OLD, WHO'S AN ADVENTURER, PART-TIME.

IT MIGHT SEEM KIND OF STRANGE, BUT YOU'VE GOTTA BELIEVE ME!

I SAY THAT I'M A PART-TIME ADVENTURER, AND THAT'S 100% TRUE. THAT'S ONLY 'CAUSE MY FULL-TIME GIG INVOLVES SOMETHING TOTALLY DIFFERENT. SOMETHING MORE ALONG THE LINES OF "KEEPING BALANCE BETWEEN WHAT IS GENERALLY CONSIDERED TO BE THE *NATURAL* AND *SUPERNATURAL* SIDES OF THINGS IN OUR MODERN-DAY SOCIETY." TO PUT IT BLUNTLY, MY JOB IS TO ACTIVELY STEP IN WHENEVER CREATURES WITH POWERS BEYOND CONVENTIONAL UNDERSTANDING CLASH WITH THOSE WHO ARE UNABLE TO STOP THEM. BUT WE'LL SPEAK MORE ON THAT IN JUST A MINUTE. THERE'S SOMEONE ELSE THAT YOU NEED TO MEET FIRST.

46

I ALREADY MAY HAVE MENTIONED THAT THIS GUY'S MY BOSS, BUT I NEVER STOPPED TO SAY HIS FULL NAME. THIS DUDE HERE IS DAVID NORTHSTAR. A WORLD-CLASS ADVENTURER...

AND AN ECCENTRIC OLD MAN WHOSE NUMBER ONE HOBBY IS FACING DOWN DANGER.

I ALREADY REVEALED HOW OLD I WAS, BUT AS FOR DAVE'S AGE, IT'S A BIT MORE COMPLICATED. YOU WOULDN'T BELIEVE ME, EVEN IF I TOLD YOU.

BUT WHO CARES? AGE IS JUST A NUMBER. AND LIKE I'VE HEARD HIM SAY, "THE KEY TO YOUTH IS TO NEVER STOP DREAMING." A LITTLE PEARL OF WISDOM, I'D SAY HAS WORKED OUT PRETTY WELL FOR HIM SO FAR.

WE FIRST MET A WHILE BACK...

AND WELL... LONG STORY, SHORT.

HE OFFERED ME A JOB AS HIS ASSISTANT...

AND I ENDED UP TAKING IT.

THAT WAS ALMOST 5 AND A HALF YEARS AGO.

47

NOW BACK TO WHAT I WAS SAYING...

THE WORLD'S A PRETTY VAST AND MYSTERIOUS PLACE. ONE WHERE ALMOST EVERYTHING YOU SEE IS NEVER ENOUGH TO SIMPLY TAKE AT FACE VALUE.

THROUGH-OUT EVERY GENERATION, THERE HAVE BEEN THOSE OUT THERE WILLING TO DO WHATEVER IT TAKES...

SO THAT NO ONE ELSE EVER REALLY HAS TO. THIS IS AN IMPORTANT AGE. ONE IN WHICH ANOMALIES EXIST AND WHERE WORLD LEADERS DO THEIR BEST TO KEEP THEM AWAY FROM THE UNSUSPECTING PUBLIC. THE BIG QUESTION IS, WHAT HAPPENS WHEN THEIR BEST JUST ISN'T ENOUGH? THAT'S WHERE WE COME IN.

WE CALL OURSELVES **THE AEON FORCE.** AN ANCIENT GROUP FOUNDED AT THE DAWN OF HISTORY TO PROTECT THOSE WHO NEED IT THE MOST.

DAVE AND I ARE JUST TWO AMONG MANY WHO HAVE BORE THIS MANTLE ACROSS COUNTLESS GENERATIONS. BUT I THINK IT'S SAFE TO SAY WE'RE ONE OF THE BEST DUOS TO EVER CARRY IT SO FAR.

48

WE'RE TASKED WITH PREVENTING STANDARD ISSUES LIKE THE THEFT OF NATURAL RESOURCES...

HEY! IT'S COOL!

AT-TEMPTED ANIMAL POACHING, AND KID-NAPPINGS.

AND MY PERSONAL FAVORITE...

DEFENDING TOWNSPEOPLE FROM PARANORMAL ANOMALIES.

THOUGH TO BE HONEST, THESE "ANOMALIES" AREN'T ANY WEIRDER THAN I AM, SO WE USUALLY GET ALONG.

HEY! YOU WANT SOME PEANUT BUTTER?

49

BESIDES, THE GENERAL IDEA IS THAT IF ANY ANIMAL'S GOING CRAZY, IT'S USUALLY 'CAUSE OF ONE OF THREE REASONS. IT'S HURT, SCARED, OR IN THIS CASE, IT'S JUST HUNGRY. AND OH YEAH! I SHOULD EXPLAIN WHY I WAS TALKING TO MYSELF AND RECORDING AUDIO BITS A LITTLE WHILE AGO.

I MAKE LITTLE SHORT STORIES BASED ON OUR ADVENTURES AND USE THE RECORDED AUDIO FOR THE DIALOGUE AND NARRATION. BUT FOR THE SAKE OF GOOD ENTERTAINMENT, I OFTEN EXAGGERATE CERTAIN EVENTS FROM TIME TO TIME. DO ME A FAVOR, AND DON'T TELL ANYONE, OKAY?

IN MY SPARE TIME, I RUN AN ANIMATED WEB SERIES.

SOA Episode 621 - Don't Push Your Luck. Push Traps Instead!

2.2M views

👍 33K   👎 2   ↗ Share   ≡+ Save   ⚑ Report

WAY BACK IN THE DAY, DAVE USED TO HOST A TV SHOW CALLED "THE SPIRIT OF ADVENTURE"...

AND FOR THE TIMES, IT WAS VERY SUCCESSFUL.

UNFORTUNATELY, IT RAN INTO SOME... "MINOR PRODUCTION ISSUES."

HAHA! CUT TO COMMERCIAL!

SO IT WAS REMOVED FROM THE NETWORK.

BUT MY SERIES IS BASICALLY ITS LOW BUDGET RENEWAL. SO, THE ADVENTURE LIVES ON!

51

FULL PAY IN USD. NICE JOB, FELLAS!

BUT FUN STUFF ASIDE, LET'S TALK BUSINESS...

YEAH! NICE JOB!

BUSINESS IS GREAT! WE MAKE REALLY GOOD MONEY.

BUT THAT'S NOT VERY SURPRISING. AS FAR AS MONSTER RELOCATION GOES, WE'RE THE ONLY REAL OPTION. WHETHER OUR CLIENT COMES FROM THE GOVERNMENT OR PRIVATE SECTOR, THIS PART OF THE JOB ALWAYS PAYS SUPER WELL!

HOWEVER, THE AEON FORCE HAS NEVER DONE ANY OF THIS STUFF FOR THE MONEY, BUT RATHER IN SPITE OF IT. GENERALLY SPEAKING, THIS STUFF'S PRETTY FUN, SO WE'D STILL DO IT WHETHER THERE WAS MONEY ATTACHED TO IT OR NOT. THE GOOD PAY IS JUST AN ADDED BONUS.

LISTEN DUDE, IF YOU HEAD NORTH, PAST THE FENCES, THERE'S THIS MAGICAL WOODEN ARCH CALLED THE TOLLAN STARGATE. IT'S TOTALLY SICK, BRO!

KNOWLEDGE IS POWER!

YO! THAT IS SICK!

BESIDES, IF YOU ASK ME, TRUE WEALTH IS MEASURED IN GOOD FRIENDS AND IN THE VALUE OF LEARNING. 'CAUSE AFTER ALL...

THOUGH THAT'S NOT TO SAY I DON'T APPRECIATE THE MONEY. I REALLY DO, IT'S JUST THAT WHAT EXCITES ME MOST ABOUT IT ISN'T HOW I SPEND IT ON MYSELF.

THE THING IS, BACK HOME I HAVE TWO YOUNGER SIBLINGS. AND GROWING UP, MY FAMILY AND I DIDN'T EXACTLY HAVE MUCH. I STILL HAD AN AMAZING CHILDHOOD, AND MY PARENTS MADE IT AS AWESOME FOR ME AS THEY COULD, SO I AM GRATEFUL FOR THAT. STILL, I HAD MY FAIR SHARE OF STRUGGLES THAT I WOULDN'T WANT ANYONE ELSE TO REPEAT. SO TO MAKE LIFE A BIT EASIER FOR ALL OF THEM, I SEND MOST OF MY EARNINGS BACK AS OFTEN AS I CAN. IT'S QUITE A BIG SUM, BUT IT'S THE LEAST I COULD DO. I JUST THINK OF IT AS MY SPECIAL WAY OF LOOKING OUT FOR THEM, I GUESS.

IT'S ALSO WORTH MENTIONING THAT I'VE A *SLIGHTLY* UNHEALTHY HABIT OF DONATING EXCESS CASH TO WORTHY CHARITIES. USUALLY TO THE POINT WHERE I DON'T HAVE ENOUGH TO BUY FOOD FOR MYSELF. THOUGH LATELY, DAVE'S BEEN GIVING ME PAY RAISES TO TRY AND OFFSET THAT...

THIS MONEY IS *YOURS*, SO SPEND IT ON *YOURSELF*. GO BUY SOME FOOD. YOU'RE TOO THIN!

"GRANDPA" MODE ACTIVATED!

UGHH

OK...

BUT I'M OFTEN TEMPTED TO DONATE THOSE TOO.

DAVE ON THE OTHER HAND, DOESN'T WORRY ABOUT MONEY VERY MUCH.

HE MADE HIS FORTUNE BY SELLING ARTIFACTS THAT USED TO BELONG TO ROYALTY. AND THANKS TO THAT, HE'S WEALTHIER THAN ANY ROYAL IN HISTORY. WHAT AN INSPIRATION!

HE'S ALSO A GUY WHO SAYS WEIRD STUFF LIKE THIS A LOT...

WHAT AN INSPIRATION!

HEHEHE! MY GRAND-IOSE PLAN FOR THIS WORLD...

IS GONNA COST A HECK OF A LOT MORE THAN ANYTHING MONEY ALONE COULD EVER HOPE TO BUY!

TRUTH BE TOLD, BEFORE I REALLY KNEW THE GUY, I THOUGHT HE WAS LIKE AN OLD CARTOON VILLAIN WITH A SCHEME FOR WORLD DOMIN-ATION.

BUT LUCKILY, I REALIZED THAT HIS PLAN FOR THE WORLD WAS SOMETHING FAR MORE NOBLE AND FAR LESS DASTARDLY THAN I'D INITIALLY THOUGHT.

—TO SUM IT UP, WHAT HE'S TRYING TO DO FOR THE WORLD IS MAKE IT WELCOMING AGAIN FOR AN OLD SET OF FRIENDS THAT HUMANITY SURE OWES A LOT TO.

THOUGH I'D RATHER NOT GO INTO ANOTHER FLASHBACK TO DESCRIBE IT ALL JUST YET. SO I HOPE A BRIEF HISTORY LESSON CAN DO THEM ALL JUSTICE.

LONG AGO, HUMANITY FIRST MET A GROUP OF KIND-HEARTED TRAVELERS WHO ARRIVED ON OUR PLANET FROM A WORLD FAR, FAR AWAY. MOST MODERN HISTORIANS KNOW VERY LITTLE ABOUT THEM, COURTESY OF A CERTAIN SOMEONE I WILL GLADLY POINT FINGERS AT LATER. BUT ANYWAY, TO ANCIENT HUMANS, THEY WERE SPECIAL, WITH MANY OF THEM BELIEVING THAT THE MYTHOI WERE GODS. BUT UNLIKE MOST STORIES OR MOVIES ABOUT ALIEN INVASION, THESE PEOPLE DIDN'T COME HERE TO TAKE OVER OR SUBJUGATE HUMANITY OR ANYTHING. INSTEAD, THEY JUST INTRODUCED THEMSELVES AS THE MYTHOI AND SAID THAT THEY WERE HAPPY TO BE HERE.

EVEN THOUGH MOST OF THEM WOULD'VE NEVER ADMITTED IT, THEY WERE AMAZING BEYOND BELIEF.

SO INCREDIBLE IN FACT, THAT THE WORD "MYTHOLOGY" ITSELF WAS MADE SOLELY TO HONOR THEM.

COMPARED TO THE MYTHOI, WE WEREN'T ALL THAT GREAT. THEY COULD PERFORM MIRACLES THAT SURPASSED ALL LOGIC, AND WERE REVERED BECAUSE OF IT.

EVEN SO, THEY BELIEVED IN OUR POTENTIAL, AND WERE NICE ENOUGH TO TEACH US EVERYTHING THAT THEY KNEW.

UNFORTUNATELY, OUR TIME WITH THE MYTHOI WAS CUT SHORT...

AS A VITAL ELEMENT FOR THEIR SURVIVAL HAD GONE MISSING.

THEY ENTRUSTED THEIR LEGACY TO A GROUP OF 10 DISCIPLES WHO WOULD EVENTUALLY GO ON TO FOUND THE AEON FORCE.

THE FOUNDERS TRAVELED THE WORLD HELPING OTHERS. USING THE KNOW-LEDGE ACQUIRED FROM THE MYTHOI, THEY WENT ON TO CREATE THE VARIOUS ANCIENT CIVILIZATIONS WE KNOW OF TODAY. AT ONE POINT, THEY REALIZED THAT THE BEST WAY TO PRESERVE THE MYTHOI'S TEACHINGS WAS TO COMPILE THEIR KNOWLEDGE INTO A COLLECTION OF EDUCATIONAL AND HISTORICAL TEXTS BEFORE THE INFORMATION BECAME TOO DILUTED OVER TIME.

THESE TEXTS ARE CALLED THE MYTHICHRONICLES, AS EACH ONE WAS MADE TO PASS ON UNIQUE STORIES AND LESSONS LEARNED FROM DIFFERENT MYTHOI.

HOWEVER... THE ONLY PERSON WHO EVER TRULY RECEIVED THOSE LESSONS WAS DAVE, SINCE HE'S THE ONLY ONE THAT CAN EVEN READ THEM. SIDE NOTE: HE'S EXTREMELY PROTECTIVE OF HIS COLLECTION, SO HE TAKES VERY GOOD CARE OF IT.

DARN RIGHT! THIS HERE COLLECTION'S GONNA STAY IN TIP-TOP SHAPE IF I'VE GOT ANYTHING TO SAY ABOUT IT. SO PAWS OFF!

HOWEVER, HE HAS TRANSLATED AND PUBLISHED SOME EDITIONS OF THE MYTHICHRONICLE, SO HE'S NOT KEEPING ANY SECRETS. IT'S JUST THAT MOST PEOPLE THINK THAT THEY'RE ONLY FICTIONAL STORIES, RATHER THAN LEGIT FIRST-HAND ACCOUNTS.

ASIDE FROM OLD BOOKS, POWERFUL ITEMS MADE DURING THE MYTHOI ERA STILL EXIST OUT THERE IN PRETTY LARGE QUANTITIES. IN FACT, MANY OF THESE RELICS HAVE SERVED AS THE BASIS FOR OTHER TYPES OF FICTIONAL SUPER WEAPONS AND MYSTICAL ARTIFACTS THAT HAVE APPEARED THROUGHOUT HISTORY.

A NICE LITTLE SIDE QUEST OF OURS IS TO FIND AS MANY OF THESE RELICS AS WE CAN, AND WE HAVE ABOUT TWO REASONS FOR WHY WE DO THAT. THE FIRST REASON IS TO KEEP THEM AWAY FROM PEOPLE WHO WOULD TRY AND USE THEM FOR EVIL...

AND THE SECOND REASON IS TO RESEARCH HOW THEY WORK IN ORDER TO IMPROVE MODERN SOCIETY. WHICH, IN MY HUMBLE OPINION, IS AN OVERALL PRETTY HONORABLE THING TO DO, IF YOU ASK ME.

NOW GRANTED, I AM THE SAME GUY WHO WANTED TO MAKE ANOTHER TREE-BOT FROM THE ANCIENT BATTERY I'D JUST FOUND.

BUT THAT'S ALL IN THE NAME OF SCIENCE, SO WHAT COULD POSSIBLY GO WRONG?

BUT ASIDE FROM THAT...

A BIG QUESTION MIGHT BE, "WHERE IN THE WORLD DO YOU EVEN FIND RELICS LIKE THOSE?"

THE ANSWER IS THAT YOU CAN OFTEN FIND THEM TUCKED AWAY IN REMOTE AREAS OF THE WORLD THAT ARE KEPT UNDER LOCK AND KEY BY GOVERNMENTS AND PRIVATE LAND OWNERS. SO IN ADDITION TO GETTING PAID FOR OUR SERVICES, WE'RE ALSO GRANTED SPECIAL ACCESS TO PLACES LIKE THESE THAT ARE OTHERWISE OFF LIMITS TO THE PUBLIC DUE TO HIGH LEVELS OF SUPERNATURAL ACTIVITY.

HI MOM!

SO BEHOLD!

THE LOST CITY OF AURELIA.

IT MIGHT NOT LOOK LIKE MUCH ANYMORE, BUT AURELIA WAS ONCE AN ANCIENT CENTER OF SOCIETAL GROWTH AND DEVELOPMENT THE LIKES OF WHICH THE WORLD HAD NEVER YET SEEN BEFORE. IT WAS THE FIRST MODERN CITY HUMANS EVER HAD A HAND IN CREATING AND THE ONE THAT ALMOST NOBODY KNOWS ABOUT. THAT'S BECAUSE IT WAS SEALED OFF AND ABANDONED THOUSANDS OF YEARS AGO. WHICH WAS IN RETROSPECT, PROBABLY THE REASON WHY IT GOT LOST IN FIRST PLACE.

WE OFTEN CLASSIFY LOCATIONS LIKE THESE AS R.O.O.T. SITES. WITH THE WORD "ROOT" BEING A SIMPLE ACRONYM THAT MEANS A SITE IS ONE HOUSING THE "REMNANTS OF OTHERWORLDLY TECHNOLIGIES." COUPLED WITH THE FACT THAT THESE LOCATIONS ARE PHYSICALLY LOCKED DOWN AND PROTECTED, THEY ALSO COME WITH A STRANGE SET OF LORE MEANT TO DETER SPINELESS INTRUDERS. IN AURELIA'S CASE, WE HAD THAT GHOST STORY, WHICH WAS JUST ONE EXAMPLE OF THE MANY RUMORS AND LEGENDS MADE UP TO KEEP THE WRONG PEOPLE OUT.

BUT NO MATTER HOW COOL THE LEGENDS OR FANTASIES MAY SEEM, THE COLD HARD TRUTH IS ALWAYS FAR MORE INTERESTING.

TAKE IT FROM THE NUMBER ONE MYTHOI RELIC RESEARCHER ON THE PLANET, EVERYTHING YOU SEE AT FIRST GLANCE IS JUST THE TIP OF THE ICEBERG.

YOU NEVER KNOW WHAT ANY OF THEM CAN TRULY DO UNTIL YOU PUT IN THE TIME TO FIGURE THAT OUT.

TAKE THESE GOGGLES, FOR EXAMPLE. APPEARANCE-WISE, THEY SEEM FAIRLY NORMAL. BUT AS YOU ALREADY KNOW, THEY'RE NOT NORMAL AT ALL.

I FOUND THESE AT A R.O.O.T. SITE NEAR THE MONTEROZZI NECROPOLIS. TURNS OUT THAT IF YOU WANT TO HIDE SOMETHING GOOD, HIDING IT IN THE SAME PLACE YOU PUT A BUNCH OF DEAD PEOPLE IS A GOOD PLACE TO START.

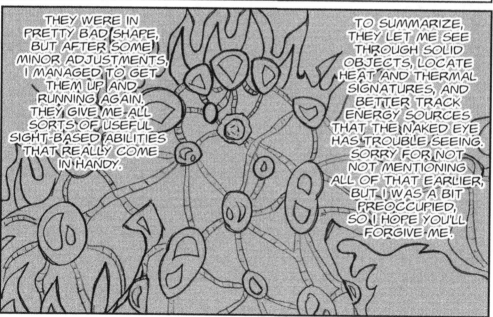

THEY WERE IN PRETTY BAD SHAPE, BUT AFTER SOME MINOR ADJUSTMENTS, I MANAGED TO GET THEM UP AND RUNNING AGAIN. THEY GIVE ME ALL SORTS OF USEFUL SIGHT-BASED ABILITIES THAT REALLY COME IN HANDY.

TO SUMMARIZE, THEY LET ME SEE THROUGH SOLID OBJECTS, LOCATE HEAT AND THERMAL SIGNATURES, AND BETTER TRACK ENERGY SOURCES THAT THE NAKED EYE HAS TROUBLE SEEING. SORRY FOR NOT NOT MENTIONING ALL OF THAT EARLIER, BUT I WAS A BIT PREOCCUPIED, SO I HOPE YOU'LL FORGIVE ME.

AND THOUGH I'M NOT MUCH OF AN ADVOCATE FOR *TOMB RAIDING*, I'LL ADMIT THAT SOMETIMES THE ENDS DO JUSTIFY THE MEANS.

BUT WHO KNOWS? MAYBE THIS ONE HERE COULD TURN OUT TO BE A NEW FAVORITE. WE'LL JUST HAVE TO WAIT AND SEE.

IN ADDITION TO THE TWO I HAVE NOW, THERE ARE MANY OTHERS CURRENTLY BEING HELD IN A HIGH SECURITY VAULT BACK IN ONE OF DAVE'S MANSIONS.

THE REASON FOR THAT IS BECAUSE THERE HAPPEN TO BE QUITE A FEW THAT ARE JUST TOO POWERFUL TO BE USED IN A CASUAL SETTING, SO WE REFRAIN FROM CARRYING ANYTHING OVERLY DANGEROUS UNLESS THE SITUATION DEMANDS IT.

THOUGH I'M PERFECTLY CONTENT JUST STICKING WITH MY GOGGLES, THERE IS ONE OTHER RELIC I'VE ALWAYS WANTED TO TRY OUT FOR MYSELF.

HEY, YOU KNOW I COULD GET US THERE A WHOLE LOT QUICKER IF YOU JUST LET ME USE THE TELE-PORTER, RIGHT?

TELEPORTER? OHO, WAIT! DO YOU MEAN... THE NORTHSTAR?!

SURE.

HAHA! WELL WHY DIDN'T YA SAY SO?!

BEHOLD! THE NORTHSTAR! A MARVELOUS DEVICE THAT I NAMED AFTER YOURS TRULY!

WITH THIS LITTLE GIZMO, I CAN INSTANTLY TRANSPORT MYSELF AND A MAXIMUM OF 20 OTHERS TO ANY LOCATION I ENVISION IN MY MIND!

TRULY AN ASSET TO ANY TRAVELER SEEKING TO SKIP OUT ON AIRFARE, AND AN ABSOLUTELY PERFECT TOOL TO USE IN OUR SPECIFIC SITUATION!

BUT WE'RE NOT GONNA USE IT!!

WHY?!

ANYWAYS... WHAT I WANTED TO SHOW YOU IS DOWN THERE.

OHO, INTERESTING! THIS HUGE PROPAGATING CRACK IN THE GROUND... WAS IT HERE WHEN YOU ARRIVED OR DID YOU MAKE IT YOURSELF?

MAY I ASK HOW?

WELL... I MADE IT MYSELF.

THAT'S HOW.

THE HECK DOES THAT MEAN?

I FIGURED YOU'D SAY THAT.

YOU SEE, WHEN I GOT HERE I NOTICED A ROOT FROM THE CEILING WAS DRIPPING FLUID DIRECTLY ONTO AN "X" MARKED SPOT ON THE GROUND...

IN THIS CASE, "X" QUITE LITERALLY MARKED THE SPOT FOR ME.

DRRIP

HEAVY EXPLANATION: INCOMING!

AND THEN I LOOKED OVER AT THE GIANT STONE SNAKE MONSTER, AND SAW THAT IT HAD A FLASK OF ACID PERCHED IN ITS MOUTH. NEEDLESS TO SAY, IT WAS QUITE OBVIOUS WHAT IT WAS THERE FOR.

64

I KNEW I HAD TO GET TO IT, BUT THIS WAS CLEARLY A PUZZLE THAT I NEEDED TO OUTSMART BEFORE I COULD FULFILL THAT OBJECTIVE. THE FIRST PECULIAR OBSERVATION I MADE WAS THAT THERE WERE MECHANICAL HINGES OVERTOP OF THE SNAKE'S JAW JOINTS. WHICH IN MY EXPERIENCE, IS A DEAD GIVEAWAY THAT WHAT I WAS DEALING WITH WAS THE CLASSIC, "DUNGEON KEY SITTING ON A PRESSURE PLATE IN THE MONSTER'S MOUTH, THAT'LL BITE YOUR HAND OFF IF YOU DONT REPLACE IT WITH AN OBJECT OF AT LEAST AN EQUIVALENT WEIGHT" TRICK. BUT IN TRUTH, IT'S A RUN-OF-THE-MILL CLASSIC THAT'S EASY TO BEAT WITH SOME SIMPLE CALCULATIONS.

THE FIRST THING I DID WAS ASSUME THAT THE FLASK WAS MADE OF A MATERIAL OF SIMILAR PROPERTIES TO STAINLESS STEEL. BECAUSE OF ITS CORROSION RESISTANCE, IT'S THE BEST CONTAINER FOR MOST KINDS OF ACIDS. NEXT, I GOT THE DIMENSIONS FOR THE CONTAINER, INCLUDING THE CAP IN INCHES, AND ESTIMATED THAT THE WALLS OF THE FLASK WERE A QUARTER OF AN INCH THICK. THEN, I STARTED TO CALCULATE THE OVERALL VOLUME OF THE FLASK ITSELF, WHILE ASSUMING THAT THE INSIDE OF IT WAS HOLLOW.

THE VOLUME OF THE FLASK CAME OUT TO BE ABOUT 9.8 CUBIC INCHES, BUT SINCE OFF THE TOP OF MY HEAD, I ONLY KNEW THAT THE DENSITY OF STAINLESS STEEL IS AROUND 7.93 GRAMS PER CUBIC CENTIMETERS, I CONVERTED THE UNITS AND MULTIPLIED TO GET A WEIGHT OF ABOUT 1273.08 GRAMS, WHICH IS ABOUT THE EQUIVALENT OF 2.81 POUNDS. NEXT, I ASSUMED THAT THE ACID INSIDE OF THE FLASK WAS EITHER PHOSPHORIC ACID OR TRISODIUM PHOSPHATE, SINCE THEY'RE USED TO DISSOLVE CONCRETE, WHICH FELT VERY SIMILAR TO THIS FLOOR FOR SOME REASON. THOUGH, I HIGH-BALLED MY CALCULATIONS FOR PHOSPHORIC ACID SINCE ITS DENSITY OF 1.88 GRAMS PER CUBIC CENTIMETER IS GREATER THAN TRISODIUM PHOSPHATE'S DENSITY OF 1.62. USING THE DIMENSIONS FOR ONLY THE INSIDE OF THE FLASK, I CALCULATED THAT THE WEIGHT OF THE ACID WAS 1108.71 GRAMS, SO ROUGHLY 2.44 POUNDS.

CLICK
CLICK
CLICK

THEN, ALL I DID WAS ADD THOSE WEIGHTS TOGETHER AND GOT 5.25 POUNDS AS ITS TOTAL WEIGHT. SOON AFTER THAT, I FILLED UP A BAG WITH A BIT OVER 6 POUNDS OF DIRT, JUST IN CASE I WAS SLIGHTLY OFF WITH SOME OF MY ASSUMPTIONS. AND THEN I JUST SWAPPED IT OUT FOR THE FLASK OF ACID, AND VOILA! I GOT TO KEEP MY HAND.

GOTCHA!

HEAVY EXPLANATION: COMPLETE!

I FINISHED THINGS OFF BY POURING OUT THE ACID ONTO THE "X" MARK, AND WAITED TO SEE WHAT WOULD HAPPEN.

IT DIDN'T TAKE LONG FOR THAT CRACK TO SPREAD, AND EVENTUALLY, I DISCOVERED A HIDDEN BASEMENT. SIMPLE AS THAT.

HISSSSS   HISSSSS

BUT WHAT I FOUND DOWN THERE NEXT WAS DEFINITELY THE HIGHLIGHT OF EVERY-THING.

BUT YOU'LL JUST HAVE TO WAIT AND SEE FOR-

HUH?

ADVENTURE WAITS FOR NO ONE!!!

HEY!!! WHAT THE HECK?! DID YOU JUST ASK A QUESTION, AND THEN *NOT* LISTEN TO A SINGLE THING I HAD TO SAY IN REPONSE TO IT?!?!?!

YOU BET! YOU WERE TOO WORDY!

TOO WORDY?!

WELL, PARDON ME FOR TRYING TO PROVIDE A DETAILED EXPLANATION!

AND HEY! "ADVENTURE WAITS FOR NO ONE" IS MY LINE! I'M THE ONE WHO CAME UP WITH IT!

67

BUT CASTING ASIDE MY OWN PERSONAL NAUSEA, THIS ISN'T EXACTLY WHAT I BROUGHT YOU HERE TO SEE.

NO, INSTEAD IT'S WHATEVER THIS THING WAS GUARDING THAT I NEED YOU TO TAKE A LOOK AT.

I COULD GO INTO ENRICHING DETAIL ABOUT EVERYTHING AGAIN, BUT YOU'RE FAR TOO IMPATIENT FOR THAT.

GASP!

SO I'LL JUST SKIP THE EXPLANATION AND TAKE YOU STRAIGHT TO IT.

EXCELLENT!!! NOW THAT'S WHAT I LIKE TO HEAR!

WELP, HERE WE ARE. ANY IDEA WHAT THIS IS?

HO!

OH!

HO!

ALEX, MY BOY! DO YOU HAVE ANY IDEA WHAT THE MYTHOLOGICAL MARVEL YOU'VE FOUND HERE TODAY IS?!

NOPE. THAT'S WHY I JUST ASKED.

THAT, MY FRIEND! IS NONE OTHER THAN THE FABLED **CAULDRON OF COALESCENCE!!!**

WHY DO I GET THE FEELING THAT YOU JUST MADE THAT NAME UP?

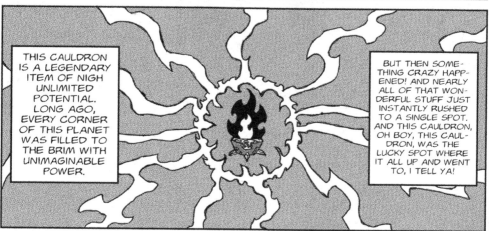

THIS CAULDRON IS A LEGENDARY ITEM OF NIGH UNLIMITED POTENTIAL. LONG AGO, EVERY CORNER OF THIS PLANET WAS FILLED TO THE BRIM WITH UNIMAGINABLE POWER.

BUT THEN SOMETHING CRAZY HAPPENED! AND NEARLY ALL OF THAT WONDERFUL STUFF JUST INSTANTLY RUSHED TO A SINGLE SPOT. AND THIS CAULDRON, OH BOY, THIS CAULDRON, WAS THE LUCKY SPOT WHERE IT ALL UP AND WENT TO, I TELL YA!

I'VE DREAMT OF THIS MOMENT FOR SO MANY YEARS!

AND FOR ME TO FINALLY SEE IT HERE IN PERSON, IS TRULY A DREAM COME TRUE!

I'VE GOTTA TAKE IT, BUT THESE VINES ARE GETTIN' IN MY WAY!

YEAH. ABOUT THAT...

RIP!

YEET!

I'M NOT TOO SURE WHY, BUT THE THOUGHT OF TAKING IT FROM HERE...

JUST SEEMS LIKE A *REALLY BAD* IDEA TO ME, ALL OF A SUDDEN.

WE PUT A LOT OF EFFORT INTO MAKING SURE DANGEROUS ITEMS LIKE THESE *DON'T* GO CAUSING A BUNCH OF TROUBLE, AND WELL, CALL IT A HUNCH, BUT...

UNLIKE THE OTHERS WE'VE FOUND OVER THE YEARS, I THINK THIS ONE IS A TREASURE THAT WAS *MEANT* TO STAY BURIED.

OOH! INTENSE STARE YA GOT THERE. I LIKE IT! BUT TRUST ME, ALEX. BETWEEN THE TWO OF US, WE HAVE NOTHING TO WORRY ABOUT.

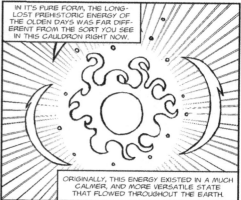

IN IT'S PURE FORM, THE LONG-LOST PREHISTORIC ENERGY OF THE OLDEN DAYS WAS FAR DIFFERENT FROM THE SORT YOU SEE IN THIS CAULDRON RIGHT NOW.

ORIGINALLY, THIS ENERGY EXISTED IN A MUCH CALMER, AND MORE VERSATILE STATE THAT FLOWED THROUGHOUT THE EARTH.

BUT WHEN LOTS OF IT CAME RUSHING TOGETHER ALL THOSE YEARS AGO, SOMETHING BRAND NEW WAS CREATED. AT THAT TIME, A POWERFUL AND INTENSE ENERGY THAT THE ANCIENTS CALLED VANTICHOR WAS BORN.

BY ITSELF, VANTICHOR'S NOT THAT BAD. IT'S ONLY THE COMBINATION OF COUNTLESS OTHER ENERGIES ALL MELDED TOGETHER. IT IS SORT OF CREEPY TO LOOK AT THOUGH, SO I GET YOUR CONCERNS!

BUT ANY POWER IS ONLY GOOD OR BAD DEPENDING ON WHOEVER'S USIN' IT, ANYWAY.

AND I THINK WE'RE A COUPLE OF DECENT GUYS WHO CAN MAKE A WHOLE LOTTA GOOD COME OUT OF THIS, LONG TERM. WOULDN'T YOU AGREE?

WITH THIS POWER, WE CAN RESTORE THE WORLD! WE CAN BRING BACK ITS LOST POTENTIAL FOR *EVERYONE* TO ENJOY AGAIN! IN ITS CURRENT STATE, THE CAULDRON'S USELESS TO US. BUT IF WE SEPARATE ITS ENERGY BACK INTO ITS ORIGINAL FORMS, WE CAN RE-DELIVER THEM TO THE WORLD, AND SET THINGS RIGHT! YOU'VE JUST GOTTA TRUST ME! I'VE GOT A FOOLPROOF PLAN ALL READY TO GO!

HRK

HRK

HRK

GAH!!! H-HIS HAIR'S ON FIRE!!!

I'VE BEEN THINKIN' OF THIS PLAN FOR QUITE A WHILE NOW AND I'M PRETTY DARN PROUD OF IT...

PHEW...

BUT I'M A ONE MAN ARMY, NOT A ONE MAN ENCYCLOPEDIA. SO I'LL NEED YOUR SMARTS TO ENSURE OUR SUCCESS, SHOULD I GOOF THINGS UP!

BUT WITH OUR COMBINED SKILLS THERE'S NO WAY WE COULD FAIL. SO WHADDYA SAY, ALEX? ARE YOU IN?

THANK YOU, ALEX. LIKE I SORTA SAID, YOU'RE THE KEY TO OUR SUCCESS IF THINGS GO AWRY. I'M COUNTIN' ON YA, KID!

IT'S AGAINST MY BETTER JUDGEMENT, BUT I CAN'T EXACTLY STOP YOU. SO, YEAH. I'M IN. YOU'LL DEFINITELY NEED MY HELP, THAT'S FOR SURE.

YEAH. SO IN OTHER WORDS, THIS'LL BE MY PROBLEM TO FIX IF SOMETHING GOES WRONG... RIGHT?

EXACTLY! NOW LET'S GET OUTTA HERE!!

ADVENTURE WAITS FOR NO ONE!!!

FWSHH

BOING!

JERICHO Inc.

LETHAL STORAGE & MORE.

THE THING IS THOUGH, WE ENDED UP NOT HOLDING ON TO THE CAULDRON FOR VERY LONG.

??

C'MON JERKO...

IT'S JERICHO!

JERKO, JERICHO, WHATEVER! YOU HAVE THE BEST FACILITIES IN THE WORLD! YOU SHOULD HOLD ONTO IT.

GRR. FINE. BUT THIS HAD BETTER NOT BE ANOTHER ONE OF YOUR TRICKS, NORTHSTAR.

YEAH, SURE... BUT FIRST, YOU'LL NEED TO SIGN SOME WAIVERS.

HAHA! WHAT A STEAL!

WHICH CONFUSED ME A LOT, CONSIDERING DAVE HANDED IT OVER TO SOME GUY HE TOLD ME HE HATED BEFORE.

HEY DUDE, WHAT GIVES? I THOUGHT YOU HATED THAT GUY.

HAHA! YOU BET I DO!

BUT HE ELABORATED MORE ON WHY HE DECIDED TO DO THAT, NOT LONG AFTER IT SHIPPED. AND NEEDLESS TO SAY, I WAS SILENTLY OPPOSED.

UH... HI!

THIS WILL CHANGE THE WORLD!

USUALLY, WE TEND TO KEEP OUR ACCOMPLISHMENTS QUIET. BUT THIS TIME, DAVE DECIDED TO REALLY OVERHYPE THINGS AND PUBLICIZE OUR DISCOVERY AS MUCH AS POSSIBLE.

YEAH, YOU KNOW. THIS IS LIKE, THE SINGLE MOST IMPORTANT DISCOVERY EVER. JUST SAYIN'.

I LOVE YOUR BELT! WHO MADE IT?

OH! UM... ACTUALLY I MADE IT TO CARRY AROUND SUPPLIES EASIER.

REALLY? THAT'S SO COOL!

HEHE, THANKS!

THOUGH I'LL ADMIT. THE ATTENTION WAS SORT OF NICE FOR A CHANGE.

I HAD SOME TIME OFF FOR A BIT, AND DIDN'T KNOW WHAT TO DO...

SO INSTEAD OF MY USUAL ROUTINE, I DID SOMETHING NORMAL FOR ONCE AND WENT FOOD SHOPPING IN-STEAD.

AND DURING THAT TIME, SOME KIDS NOTICED ME FROM SPIRIT OF ADVENTURE AND ASKED FOR MY AUTOGRAPH. BEST DAY OFF EVER!

TO BE HONEST, I'VE NEVER BEEN ONE TO PURPOSELY SEEK OUT RECOGNITION. BUT THERE DEFINITELY IS SOMETHING VERY SPECIAL IN REALIZING THAT THERE ARE PEOPLE OUT THERE...

WHO AT LEAST SEEM TO THINK THAT THE THINGS I DO ARE ACTUALLY KIND OF... COOL, YOU KNOW?

75

THE PUBLICITY FROM THE CAULDRON'S DISCOVERY WAS EXCELLENT FOR BOTH DAVE AND I. LIKE I SAID, I DON'T DO THINGS FOR RECOGNITION, SO I PRETTY MUCH SHARED ALL THE CREDIT FOR FINDING IT, TO THE POINT WHERE EVERYONE ASSUMED THAT DAVE WAS THE ONE MOST RESPONSIBLE FOR UNEARTHING IT IN THE FIRST PLACE. BUT HONESTLY... I DIDN'T CARE ABOUT THAT AT ALL.

DESPITE ALREADY BEING WILDLY SUCCESSFUL, DAVE DID STILL HAVE SOME CRITICS WHO DOUBTED HIS PUBLIC CREDIBILITY AFTER THE ORIGINAL VERSION OF SPIRIT OF ADVENTURE WAS DISCONTINUED FROM TV. BUT IN JUST A FEW SHORT DAYS, HE'D TOLD THE NAYSAYERS TO PUT A SOCK IN IT, AND BECAME A GLOBAL SENSATION ALL OVER AGAIN. AND FRANKLY, I JUST COULDN'T HELP BUT FEEL HAPPY FOR THE GUY.

BUT YOU KNOW, IN LIFE IT'S IMPORTANT TO APPRECIATE THE GOOD TIMES AS THEY COME, BUT TO ALSO REMEMBER NOT TO LOSE YOURSELF TOO GREATLY IN THE EUPHORIA. NOW, THAT DOESN'T MEAN YOU HAVE TO GROUND YOURSELF SO MUCH THAT YOU FORGET TO ENJOY THE HIGHS THAT COME YOUR WAY, BUT IT DOES MEAN THAT YOU CAN'T LET YOUR HEAD GET STUCK SO FAR IN THE CLOUDS THAT YOU FAIL TO SEE THE STORM THAT IS BREWING AROUND YOU.

OCTOBER 15TH

BUT TRUTH BE TOLD, THAT WASN'T QUITE THE CASE.

JERICHO INC. FACILITIES. OUTSIDE OF DENVER, CO, USA.

AND THE ENCROACHING STORM WAS ONE WE HAD PREPARED FOR, WELL IN ADVANCE.

9:52 AM

BUT UNFORTUNATELY, NO ONE...

COULD PREDICT THE SEVERITY OF THE EVENTS YET TO COME.

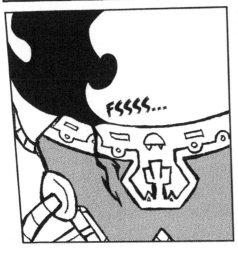

FSSSS...

GRSSH!!

CHAPTER 2, END.

ADVENTURER'S NOTES #2

HERE TO OUR LEFT, WE CAN SEE THE TOLLAN STARGATE. I DIDN'T GET THE CHANCE TO TALK MUCH ABOUT IT BEFORE, SO I FIGURED I SHOULD COME BACK TO IT. I DIDN'T REALLY GO OVER THIS WITH OUR FIRST ENTRY, BUT I'LL BE USING MY ADVENTURER'S NOTES AS A WAY TO EXPAND ON SOME SUBJECTS I MAY NOT HAVE FULLY COVERED. I HOPE YOU'LL ENJOY!

BUT WITH THAT OUT OF THE WAY, LET'S GET BACK TO THE STARGATE! THE TOLLAN STARGATE IS ONE OF MANY SPECIAL TYPES OF BARRIERS THAT CAN ALTER THE FLOW OF SPACE ITSELF! IT WAS MADE TO CONCEAL AURELIA IN ITS OWN POCKET DIMENSION AS A MEANS OF CONTAINING THE CITY'S MYSTERIOUS AURA. BARRIERS LIKE THESE CAN ONLY BE BREACHED IN RESPONSE TO AN INCREDIBLY POWERFUL PRESENCE.

ALSO, ANOTHER HIDDEN LANDMARK THAT'S WORTHY OF MENTIONING IS THE GREAT SORAYA, OTHERWISE KNOWN AS "THE TREE OF GREAT SORROW." USUALLY TREES OF THIS VARIETY ARE JUST CALLED SORAYAS, OR "TREES OF SORROW." BUT SINCE THIS ONE'S SO MUCH BIGGER THAN HOW THEY'RE NORMALLY SUPPOSED TO BE, I'D SAY IT'S PLENTY DESERVING OF BEING CALLED GREAT! LIVING UP TO THEIR NAME, TREES OF SORROW CONSISTENTLY DRIP TEAR-LIKE SAP FROM THEMSELVES AND HAVE AN OVERALL APPEARANCE THAT JUST SCREAMS "DOOM AND GLOOM", BUT WHAT THEY ACTUALLY DO FOR THE SURROUNDING ECOSYSTEM'S REALLY QUITE POSITIVE!

SORAYAS HAVE THE UNIQUE ABILITY TO STORE AND REDISTRIBUTE LARGE QUANTITIES OF ENERGY AFTER REACHING A CERTAIN LEVEL OF MATURITY. THEY DON'T NEED SUNLIGHT TO GROW, BUT RATHER CREATE NUTRIENTS FOR THEMSELVES BY SYNTHESIZING FOOD FROM A SEPARATE ENERGY SOURCE. ONCE ENOUGH POWER IS ABSORBED BY THE TREE, IT SPREADS ITS ROOTS AS FAR AS IT CAN TO SLOWLY RELEASE EXCESS POWER BACK INTO THE NEARBY ENVIRONMENT.

THE GREAT SORAYA IS AN EXTREME EXAMPLE OF THIS. IT HAS SLOWLY ABSORBED AND REDISTRIBUTED A SMALL PORTION OF POWER FROM THE CAULDRON OVER THE LAST SEVEN MILLENNIA. THE SPECIFIC REASON FOR WHY IT WAS PLANTED HERE REMAINS A MYSTERY, BUT THE RESTORATIVE EFFECTS IT HAS PROVIDED TO AURELIA'S HABITAT LEADS ME TO BELIEVE THAT IT WAS PLACED HERE TO SERVE A MUCH HIGHER PURPOSE.

AEON FORCE

CHAPTER 3: THE DUSK OF A NEW AGE

CHAPTER 3: THE DUSK OF A NEW AGE

GRAGH! GRAGH!

IT APPEARS AS THOUGH THE INSTRUMENT OF MY IMPRISONMENT... HAS REWARDED MY STAY WITH A NEWLY FORMED BODY...

83

DALLAS, TX, USA.

9:55 AM

ACHOOOO!!!

SHEESH! IS SOMEBODY OUT THERE TALKIN' ABOUT ME? MAYBE! I WOULDN'T BE SURPRISED.

SURE, KID. GO FOR IT.

HEY DAVE, CAN I ASK YOU FOR SOME ADVICE?

IS THIS ENOUGH HAIR GEL OR DO YOU THINK I SHOULD USE MORE?

HAHA! WELL, IF YOUR GOAL'S TO LOOK LIKE A FULLY-FLEDGED JERSEY-BOY, THEN JUST GO AHEAD AND USE THE WHOLE BOTTLE!

I MEAN... IF THE SHOE FITS.

I FIGURED I'D TRY STYLING IT A BIT SO I'D LOOK MORE PRESENTABLE, BUT I PROBABLY SHOULD HAVE JUST GOTTEN A HAIRCUT INSTEAD.

HONESTLY, I'M AMAZED BY HOW CONFIDENT YOU ARE IN THESE TYPES OF SITUATIONS. RIGHT NOW, IT FEELS LIKE NO MATTER WHAT I TRY, I JUST CAN'T HELP FEELING NERVOUS AND UN-COMFORTABLE.

TRUE CONFIDENCE, OR AT LEAST THE KIND THAT I'VE GOT AIN'T BASED ON SOMETHIN' AS SIMPLE AS APPEARANCE. NO, IT COMES FROM SOME PLACE ELSE.

YEAH, I KNOW! MY CONFIDENCE IS PRETTY DARN AMAZING, ISN'T IT? BUT YA KNOW WHAT, KID? I'LL LET YOU IN ON A LITTLE SECRET...

SO IF YA DRAW STRENGTH FROM THE THINGS YOU'VE DONE THAT MAKE YOU WHO YOU ARE, AND YOUR WORDS REALLY SPEAK TO THAT... THEN EVERYONE'LL BE TOO BUSY BEING AMAZED BY YOU TO EVEN CARE WHAT YA LOOK LIKE. IT'S AWESOME!

MY CONFIDENCE COMES FROM REMEMBERING MY ACHIEVE-MENTS. I THINK OF ALL THE COOL THINGS I'VE DONE AND REALIZE THAT MY PER-SPECTIVE HOLDS QUITE A LOT OF VALUE.

YEAH, WELL... TO BE HONEST WITH YOU, I'M NOT AS AMAZING AS YOU ARE. SO IT'LL BE A BIG CHALLENGE FOR ME TO PULL OFF THAT ACT.

IT ISN'T AN ACT, DUDE. IT'S THE REAL DEAL. AND BESIDES, I'VE SEEN YOU RISK YOUR LIFE ALL TO SAVE SOMEONE ELSE'S MORE TIMES THAN I CAN COUNT. YOU'RE JUST AS AMAZING AS I AM.

PERHAPS EVEN MORE SO!

THEN DON'T EVEN GET ME STARTED ON HOW SKILLED YOU ARE AT DISARMING TRAPS AND PUZZLES.

IN THE LAST YEAR ALONE, HOW MANY'VE YOU CRACKED SO FAR? I'VE GENUINELY LOST COUNT.

HOW MANY HAVE I CRACKED IN THE LAST YEAR SO FAR?

WELL... INCLUDING ALL OF THE ONES I TOOK CARE OF BACK AT AURELIA...

2205.

2205?!

ARE YA KIDDING ME? WITH A TRACK RECORD LIKE THAT, THERE SHOULDN'T BE A DOUBT IN YOUR MIND ABOUT HOW GREAT YOU ARE, HONESTLY!

YOU'RE ALREADY PLENTY AMAZING. JUST POINT YOUR CHIN UP, AND SHOW SOME CONFIDENCE, WILL YA?

TODAY IS A SPECIAL DAY, SO I NEED YA TO BE ON THE TOP OF YOUR A-GAME.

YOU AND I BOTH KNOW THAT VERY SOON, THIS WORLD IS GOING TO CHANGE FOREVER.

AND TRUTH BE TOLD, YOU'RE FAR MORE CAPABLE OF EXPLAINING THAT CHANGE THAN SOMEONE LIKE ME EVER COULD.

BESIDES, YOU'VE BEEN PREPARING HARD, SO I'M SURE YOU'LL DO GREAT!

BUT IF YA GET TOO NERVOUS, YOU COULD ALWAYS TRY SWITCHING TO HOW YA SPEAK IN YOUR LITTLE RE-CORDINGS. THOSE ALWAYS SEEM TO GO OVER WELL!

BUT SINCE TODAY'S MORE OF AN EDUCATIONAL EVENT, I WOULDN'T GET TOO NERVOUS IF I WERE YOU. I'M ANTICIPATING A PRETTY SMALL CROWD OUT THERE, SO DON'T SWEAT IT!

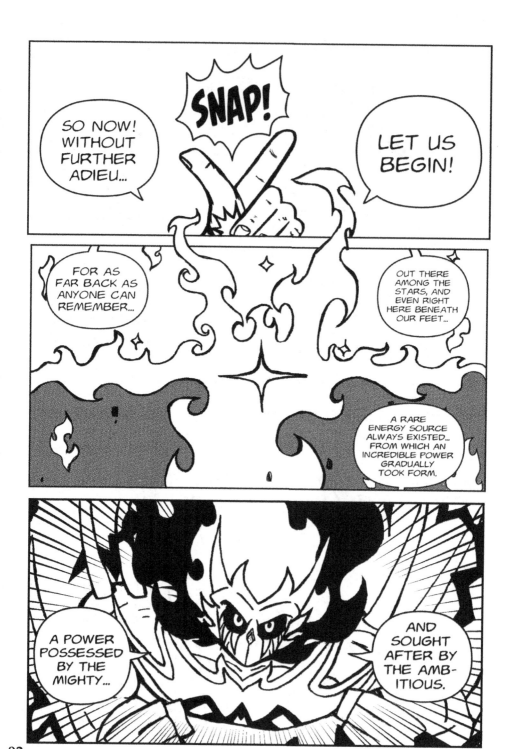

I'M THE FIRST TO ADMIT, THINGS HAVE CHANGED A LOT SINCE THE OLDEN DAYS. OH, THEY'VE CERTAINLY CHANGED A LOT! BUT THERE'S ONE THING OUT THERE THAT HAS PERSISTED THROUGHOUT EVERY GENERATION!

I'M TALKIN' ABOUT THAT GRIT, WILL-POWER, AND DETERMI-NATION...

TO SPIN ONWARD IN SPITE OF WHATEVER CRAZY TURNS FATE HAS IN STORE FOR US!

AND UNBOUND PERSISTANCE... IT'S IN EVERY-ONE! SO...

THAT POTEN-TIAL...

"MAY THE BRILLIANT WONDER BEHIND WHAT WILL BE REVEALED TODAY...

GUIDE YOU AT LAST TOWARDS YOUR JOURNEY SOON TO COME!"

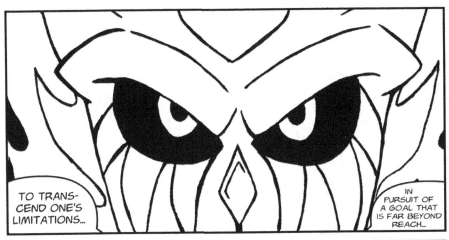

TO TRANS-CEND ONE'S LIMITATIONS...

IN PURSUIT OF A GOAL THAT IS FAR BEYOND REACH...

CERTAINLY DOES FEEL LIKE A HUMAN TRAIT, AFTER ALL!

ALTHOUGH FOR SOMEONE LIKE ME, THAT IS NO SURPRISE.

THAT FIGHT TOWARDS THE SURFACE AGAINST THE SHADOWS OF THE BLOOMED.

GRANDIOSE DREAMS ARE THE SEEDS OF TRUE PRO-GRESS...

BUT SUCH IS A VIRTUE KNOWN ONLY TO THOSE WHO HAVE BEEN HUMBLED BY PATIENCE.

BUT THE WAIT'S FINALLY OVER!

AND OH, IT SURE FELT OVERDUE!

IT WAS AN ABSENCE NOT PLANNED FOR...

BUT A RETURN THAT WAS INEVITABLE.

AND AFTER YEARS OF ANTICIPATION...

I AM OVERJOYED TO SAY...

THAT THE DAY...

I HAVE LONG AWAITED FOR...

HAS FINALLY ARRIVED!!!

THE ENERGY OF THE PAST HAS RETURNED AT LAST! AND I'M BEYOND EXCITED TO SEE ALL THAT IT CAN DO!

AND ALTHOUGH THIS LOST POWER...

HAD LEFT A WORLD WROUGHT BY RUIN...

WHEN WE WERE HANDED THAT BLANK SLATE, WE SAW IT ONLY AS A GIFT.

BECAUSE ONLY WHEN WE COME FACE TO FACE WITH THE INFINITY OF THE VOID, CAN THE LIMITLESS-NESS OF ALL WE CAN CREATE... BE TRULY UNDERSTOOD.

HAHA, YES! THANK YOU!

THANK YOU!

YOUR EXCITEMENT IS EVERYTHING!

NOW, WHILE IT'S TRUE THAT THE MORE COMPLICATED ASPECTS OF THIS STUFF ARE BEYOND OUR SCOPE FOR TODAY, WE'D BE DOING YA A DISSERVICE BY NOT AT LEAST TAKING THIS ONE STEP FURTHER.

NOW, THAT'S NOT TO SAY THAT WHAT WE'VE SPOKEN OF SO FAR HASN'T BEEN PLENTY INFORMATIVE IN ITS OWN RIGHT...

IT'S JUST THAT IF THAT WAS ALL WE CAME HERE TO SAY, THEN THE STORY'D BE INCOMPLETE, AND WE'D BE LEAVING ALL OF YOU GREAT FOLKS TOO DEEPLY IN THE DARK. AND WE WOULDN'T WANT THAT!

A NEW DISCOVERY'S BEEN MADE THAT AN AUDIENCE LIKE YOU FULLY DESERVES TO KNOW ALL ABOUT. BUT YOU'LL HAVE TO EXCUSE ME, BECAUSE I'M NOT THE TYPE OF PERSON WHO'S BEST SUITED TO DESCRIBE IT!

100

THANK YOU FOR... WHATEVER THAT WAS, DAVID. IT WAS UH.. REALLY SOMETHING ELSE.

HEY! CHIN UP, SPORT! YOU GOT THIS!

YEAH... I SURE HOPE SO.

WELL, UH... ANYWAYS, I GUESS I'LL JUST GET STARTED.

ALRIGHT, FALLING BACK ON MY PAST EXPERIENCE IS NOT GONNA WORK FOR THIS. LET'S GO FOR PLAN B...

PRETENDING THAT I'M BY MYSELF, RECORDING AN EPISODE OF SPIRIT OF ADVENTURE. I'LL JUST HAVE TO SWITCH INTO CHARACTER REAL FAST. GOSH, I HOPE THIS WORKS.

101

OKAY! SO BY NOW, YOU'VE PROBABLY GOT A PRETTY GOOD IDEA OF WHAT ANCIENT EARTH'S ECOSYSTEM MUST'VE BEEN LIKE. IT WAS DIFFERENT... BUT IN A GOOD WAY!

IT'S A PRETTY NEAT SUBJECT, THAT'S FOR SURE! BUT FROM NOW ON, WE'RE GONNA MOVE FORWARD IN A DIFFERENT DIRECTION.

AND WHILE A WONDERFUL WORLD OF THE PAST MAY SOUND INCREDIBLE... I THINK THAT THE WORLD OF THE FUTURE CAN BE JUST AS AMAZING! PERHAPS EVEN MORE SO.

LONG AGO, THESE WONDERS OF THE PAST WERE PLENTIFUL. AND OVER TIME, MEMORIES OF THEIR EXISTENCE TURNED INTO STORIES, AND FROM STORIES, TURNED INTO MYTHS, AND FROM MYTHS, TURNED INTO LEGENDS.

THESE LEGENDS INSPIRED FANTASY, AND FROM FANTASY, THE CONCEPT OF "MAGIC." AND FROM OUR FASCINATION WITH MAGIC CAME THE PURSUIT OF UNDER-STANDING THE WORLD AROUND US. SO IN OTHER WORDS... SCIENCE!

BUT FOR AS FAR BACK AS I CAN REMEMBER... MAGIC AND SCIENCE HAVE ALWAYS FELT ONE AND THE SAME!

THAT'S BECAUSE IT'S MY BELIEF THAT NO MATTER HOW MAGICAL OR EXTRAORDINARY A CONCEPT MAY INITIALLY SEEM, WITH A WHOLE-HEARTED EFFORT AND A WELL-ORGANIZED APPROACH, IT'S WITHIN OUR REACH TO MAKE SENSE OF ANYTHING!

SO BACK WHEN I FIRST LEARNED THAT THERE WAS AN ANCIENT POWER OUT THERE THAT HARDLY ANYBODY KNEW ABOUT, I MADE IT MY GOAL TO LEARN ALL THAT I COULD IN HOPES OF REVIVING A LONG-LOST FIELD OF SCIENCE SOMEDAY!!!

HEAVY EXPLANATION: INCOMING... AGAIN!

THE FIRST STEP I TOOK TO HELP ME REACH THAT GOAL WAS TO MAKE A SIMPLE OBSERVATION ABOUT A PHENOMENON IN NATURE AND COME UP WITH AN EXPERIMENT THAT'D ALLOW ME TO EXPLAIN IT. AND LUCKILY FOR ME, THE FIRST OBSERVATION I CHOSE TO EXPLORE WAS ONE I'D HAD A LOT OF EXPERIENCE WORKING WITH FOR QUITE A WHILE, IN THE FORM OF EXTREMELY RARE AND MAGNIFICENT ANOMALIES THAT HAVE UNDERGONE A PROCESS THAT I'VE RECENTLY BEGUN REFERRING TO AS *MYTHIFICATION.* BUT I'LL EXPLAIN WHAT THAT IS IN JUST A MOMENT.

FIRST, I THINK I SHOULD SAY SOME MORE ABOUT WHAT THESE ANOMALIES ARE, AND HOW THEY'RE RELATED TO ALL OF THIS IN THE FIRST PLACE. FOR STARTERS, THEY'RE BASICALLY THE SAME AS REGULAR CREATURES, EXCEPT THEY'VE UNDERGONE CERTAIN CHANGES AS A RESULT OF GRADUAL EXPOSURE TO THE PRIMORDIAL ENERGY PRESENT IN THEIR GIVEN HABITATS. NOW, MANY OF THEM HAVE BEEN AROUND FOR QUITE SOME TIME, WHILE OTHERS HAVE BEGUN POPPING UP RATHER RECENTLY. THEY'RE NOT VERY COMMON, BUT THEY'RE STILL OUT THERE. SO IF YOU HAPPEN TO HAVE A NEIGHBOR WHO'S A FAN OF CRYPTIDS OR TOLD YOU THAT THEY SAW SOME WEIRD LOOKING ANIMAL DIGGING IN THEIR GARBAGE ONCE AND YOU DIDN'T BELIEVE THEM, YOU SHOULD PROBABLY CALL THEM UP IMMEDIATELY AND APOLOGIZE. BECAUSE CHANCES ARE, THEY WERE RIGHT.

BUT ANYWAYS, BACK TO THE CONCEPT OF MYTHIFICATION. MYTH-IFICATION IS A TERM I CAME UP WITH TO DESCRIBE THE DRASTIC, BUT GRADUAL PROCESS THAT HAPPENS TO AN ORGANISM AS IT INTEGRATES POWER INTO ITS OWN BODY.

FROM WHAT I CAN GATHER, IT SEEMS THAT THESE CHANGES ARE DETERMINED BY AN ORGANISM'S ASPIRATIONS, AND CAN THUS VARY FROM INDIVIDUAL TO INDIVIDUAL.

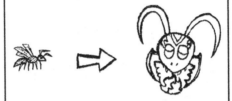

FOR EXAMPLE, I HAPPEN TO KNOW SOMEONE WHO WAS JUST A NORMAL FIRE ANT BEFORE HER MYTHIFICATION. SHE ENDED UP GROWING A LOT BIGGER, AND GAINING REAL-LIFE FIRE POWERS, TO BOOT! THE THING IS, THAT COULD'VE BEEN HER IDEA OF WHAT THE BEST VERSION OF HERSELF LOOKED LIKE, SO IT WAS LIKELY ONE OF THE FACTORS THAT INFLUENCED HER TRANSFORMATION.

KNOWING ALL OF THIS, I WANTED TO SEE WHAT WOULD HAPPEN IF SOMETHING COULD INTEGRATE POWER INTO ITSELF AT AN EVEN *FASTER* RATE THAN THE ONES SEEN IN STANDARD MYTHIFICATION. AND LUCKILY, I'D COME ACROSS A DEVICE THAT ALLOWED ME TO DO JUST THAT.

THROUGH THIS PROCESS, I LEARNED THAT THE DEVICE I'D FOUND HAD THE ABILITY TO TRANSFER BOTH ENERGY AND CONSCIOUSNESS TO THINGS THAT NORMALLY SHOULDN'T HAVE ANY...

THOUGH ADMITTEDLY, IT DID ONLY WORK ON PLANTS, AND PLANT-BASED OBJECTS FOR *SOME* REASON.

I DECIDED THAT MY TEST SUBJECTS WOULD BE A HOUSE PLANT, AN ENVELOPE, AND A PIECE OF LOOSE LEAF PAPER. THE THING IS, I QUICKLY NOTICED THAT THEY STARTED BEHAVING VERY AGGRESSIVELY TOWARDS ONE ANOTHER, NOT EVEN THAT LONG AFTER THEY WERE BASICALLY BROUGHT TO LIFE.

I WASN'T SURE AT FIRST IF THIS WAS BECAUSE OF THE FAST PACED ENERGY TRANSFER, A FUNCTION OF THE DEVICE, OR MAYBE EVEN A COMBINATION OF THE TWO. BUT KNOWING WHERE THIS DEVICE ORIGINALLY CAME FROM, I COULDN'T RULE OUT ANY IDEAS JUST YET.

GRAHH!!

AND THOUGH I'D AT FIRST STARTED THIS PROJECT FOR FAR LESS TECHNICAL REASONS THAN ONE WOULD IMAGINE... IT HELPED ME DISCOVER SOME SECRETS ABOUT THIS POWER'S BEHAVIOR THAT I'M GLAD I GOT TO LEARN.

THIS PIECE OF ANCIENT TECHNOLOGY I'D FOUND WAS... WELL, AS THE WORD ANCIENT IMPLIES, VERY, VERY OLD. SO NORMALLY, SOMETHING LIKE THIS SHOULD HAVE NEVER BEEN ABLE TO KEEP ITSELF RUNNING FOR SO LONG WITHOUT DRAWING POWER FROM A NEARBY SOURCE. SIMILARLY TO HOW A BATTERY CHARGES ITSELF, THIS DEVICE SIPHONED POWER FROM THE CAULDRON FOR YEARS, SO THE UNIT IT WAS ORIGINALLY POWERING HAD A LOT OF LOYALTY TO IT, AND WOULD ATTACK ANYTHING THAT WASN'T THE CAULDRON ITSELF. COMPARABLY, MY THREE TEST SUBJECTS BEHAVED THE SAME WAY, ALTHOUGH THEIR LOYALTY LIED A BIT... ELSEWHERE.

I GUESS SINCE I WAS THE ONE WHO GAVE THEM POWER, THEY REFUSED TO ATTACK ME...

AND INSTEAD ALL THEY DID WAS ATTACK EACH OTHER. CLEARLY, THIS WASN'T A VERY DESIRABLE RESULT... BUT IT WAS NO DOUBT A PROMISING ONE NONETHELESS.

ON THE OTHER HAND, THE CREATURES WHO RECEIVED POWER GRADUALLY FROM NATURE WEREN'T NEARLY AS AGGRESSIVE... ASSUMING THEY WERE WELL-FED AND CARED FOR, AT LEAST. GENERALLY SPEAKING, THEY WERE VERY HAPPY, AND THEIR LOYALTY WAS SOMETHING THAT HAD TO BE EARNED, JUST LIKE HOW IT'S THE CASE WITH ANYBODY ELSE, REALLY. WHICH MEANS WE GOT ALONG BECAUSE THEY THEMSELVES CHOSE TO ACCEPT ME. UNLIKE THE OTHERS, WHO I'M SURE FELT MORE OBLIGATED TO DO SO, INSTEAD.

104

OF COURSE, AT THE MOMENT, ALL OF THESE CONCEPTS ARE ONLY THEORETICAL. IT'LL TAKE A LOT MORE TESTS TO FULLY CONFIRM THEM, AND THE TAKEAWAYS MAY LIKELY ONLY APPLY TO CREATURES WHO DON'T ALREADY POSSESS ANY PARANORMAL ABILITIES PRIOR TO ENERGY EXPOSURE. UNFORTUNATELY FOR ALL OF US, THAT'S THE CATEGORY THAT MOST ACTIVE LIFE FORMS ON THIS PLANET CURRENTLY FALL INTO. BUT THANKS TO THE CAULDRON, THIS MAY NOT ALWAYS BE THE CASE.

IN MORE RECENT HISTORY, THERE HAVE ONLY EVER BEEN A HANDFUL OF LOCATIONS IN THE WORLD WHERE MYTHIFICATION IS REMOTELY POSSIBLE. EVEN THEN, IT'S A PROCESS THAT DEMANDS A HUGE AMOUNT OF EFFORT TO NATURALLY ACHIEVE. FOR THOSE TWO REASONS, IT'S AN INCREASINGLY RARE PHENOMENON FOR ANYONE TODAY TO EVEN OBSERVE.

UNFORTUNATELY, WE CAN'T MAKE THE MYTHIFICATION PROCESS ANY LESS DIFFICULT TO ACHIEVE, BUT WE CAN AT LEAST MAKE THE ENVIRONMENT SUITABLE FOR IT TO OCCUR, A LOT MORE ACCESSIBLE THAN IT CURRENTLY IS.

WITHIN THE CAULDRON LIES ALMOST ALL OF THE ENERGY THAT USED TO FLOW THROUGHOUT THE EARTH. IF WE RELEASE AND SEPARATE THE POWER THAT IT HOLDS INSIDE, WE CAN RETURN IT TO ITS RIGHTFUL PLACE AND RESTORE TONS OF AWESOME OPPORTUNITIES THAT WE'VE REALLY MISSED OUT ON OVER THE YEARS.

BUT A HISTORY OF MISSED OPPORTUNITIES IS NO FUN TO TALK ABOUT...

SO WE'LL HAVE TO SAVE THAT CHAT FOR ANOTHER DAY.

BECAUSE NOW WE HAVE SOMETHING TO LOOK FORWARD TO. SOMETHING THAT SHOULD MAKE UP FOR LOST TIME.

IN ALL OF THE TIME THAT I LOST SEALED AWAY... I NEVER STOPPED THINKING ABOUT WHAT YOU HAD SAID...

"THE STRONGEST MOTH SETTLES... FOR ONLY THE BRIGHTEST FLAME."

ONE OF MY FAVORITE QUOTES, SAID BY YOU... LONG, LONG AGO...

WHICH SIMPLY MEANS....

THAT MY OVERWHELMING POWER SHALL SERVE AS A BEACON...

WHICH WILL GUIDE YOU AT LAST TOWARDS OUR SHOWDOWN OF DESTINY.

WELL, IN CONCLUSION... THE FUTURE THAT COULD BE BORN FROM ALL OF THIS IS ASTONISHING! A FUTURE OF REMARKABLE MAGNIFICENCE AND PROPHESIED GREATNESS!

TAP!

THEN AGAIN, AT THE MOMENT, THAT MAY ONLY BE WISHFUL THINKING.

STILL, I WOULDN'T MIND SHARING HOW I *HOPE* THE FUTURE TURNS OUT SOONER OR LATER.

I HOPE THAT IN THE FUTURE, WE CREATE A WORLD THAT MATCHES THE MYSTERY AND ALLURE OF THE PAST... BUT WE MAKE SURE TO PUT OUR OWN SPIN ON IT.

HUMANITY'S COME A LONG WAY OVER THE PAST FEW THOUSAND YEARS, SO I DON'T THINK THAT WE'RE MEANT TO REPEAT ANCIENT HISTORY. BUT RATHER, LEARN FROM IT TO CREATE SOMETHING NEW!

A PLACE THAT BLENDS THE MIRACLES OF YESTERDAY WITH THE MARVELS OF TODAY!

SO, BASICALLY... A MODERN YET MAGICAL WORLD WHERE EACH OF US CAN HAVE FUN, GROW, AND DEVELOP OUR OWN UNIQUE STRENGTHS. ONE WHERE WE CAN TAKE ON NEW AND EXCITING CHALLENGES TOGETHER, IN PURSUIT OF A FUTURE THAT'S TRULY WORTH BUILDING!

IT'S AN EXCITING CONCEPT TO THINK ABOUT, BUT BELIEVE IT OR NOT, IT ISN'T UNHEARD OF. IN FACT, IT'S WHAT I THINK THAT WE, AS HUMANS, MAY ACTUALLY BE BEST AT!

SINCE THE BEGINNING OF TIME, WE'VE ALWAYS DONE OUR BEST WORK WHEN MOTIVATED BY A CAUSE THAT WE ALL TRULY BELIEVE IN.

AND FOR THIS FUTURE TO COME TRUE, I THINK THAT THIS TIME WE WE SHOULD BELIEVE IN EACH OTHER!

I KNOW THAT IT MAY NOT BE THE EASIEST ROAD TO TRAVEL DOWN, BUT SINCE WHEN HAS ACHIEVING ANYTHING WORTHWHILE... EVER REALLY BEEN EASY?

WE'RE DREAMERS, THINKERS, MAKERS, AND DOERS. WE'VE NEVER LET ANYTHING LIMIT OURSELVES BEFORE, SO WE SHOULDN'T START NOW! FOR THAT REASON, I BELIEVE IN THE FUTURE, AND SPECIFICALLY IN THE ONE THAT I KNOW WE'LL CREATE TOGETHER! SO, THANK YOU!

HEAVY EXPLANATION: COMPLETE... PHEW!

WELL DONE, KID. I KNEW YA COULD DO IT!

YEAH, WELL... I'M GLAD AT LEAST ONE OF US DID. BECAUSE FOR A WHILE THERE, I KNOW THAT I SURE DIDN'T.

HEY, UH... YOU ALRIGHT OVER THERE?

CRCK!!

GRR?!

WHO, ME? YEAH, I'M FINE! NO NEED TO WORRY!

THING IS, I JUST PICKED UP ON A CERTAIN FAMILIAR ENERGY THAT YOU AND I KNEW WOULD BE SHOWIN' UP SOONER OR LATER. SO IT LOOKS LIKE WE GOTTA SPLIT.

HE REALLY FORCED HIS WAY OUT THAT QUICKLY, HUH?

YEAH, I'M AFRAID SO. SORRY IF IT INTERRUPTS ANY CELEBRATORY PLANS THAT YA MIGHT'VE HAD.

NO, IT'S FINE. I HONESTLY DON'T HAVE ANYTHING ELSE BETTER TO DO.

THAT'S THE SPIRIT! BUT YA KNOW, WE CAN'T JUST UP AND LEAVE WITHOUT DOIN' SOMETHIN' DRAMATIC...

SO LET'S STEP OUT ON A HIGH NOTE AND SHOW THESE PEOPLE AN EXIT THAT THEY'LL NEVER FORGET!

RIGHT!

EXCUSE ME, EVERYONE. WE APOLOGIZE FOR THE SHORT NOTICE, BUT SOMETHING'S COME UP. AS A RESULT, WE'LL BE ENDING TODAY'S SHOW JUST A TAD BIT EARLY.

BUT BEFORE WE SPLIT, WE'LL DELIVER A SPECTACULAR FINALE THAT WE HOPE YOU'LL ALL ENJOY.

WHAT YOU'RE ABOUT TO SEE'S ONLY A DROP IN THE OCEAN! SO THINK OF IT AS A SAMPLE OF THE EPICNESS YET TO COME!

I'VE SAID ALL I WANTED TO, AND I'M SATISFIED FOR NOW. SO, I'LL HAND THE REINS OVER TO ALEX AND LET HIM BRING US ON HOME.

WSSH!!

111

SURE THING! HEY EVERYONE! ONCE AGAIN, THANK YOU ALL SO MUCH FOR YOUR ATTENTION TODAY. YOU WERE A REALLY GREAT CROWD! I'M SORRY THERE ISN'T ENOUGH TIME FOR A "Q AND A" SESSION. 'CAUSE AS IT STANDS, I'M SURE YOU ALL PROBABLY HAVE A MILLION TIMES MORE QUESTIONS THAN I CURRENTLY HAVE THE ANSWERS TO.

BUT THAT'S OKAY! BECAUSE IF I HAD TO SAY WHAT MY FAVORITE PART ABOUT WHAT I DO IS, I'D TELL YOU IT'S THAT THERE'S ALWAYS SOME-THING NEW OUT THERE WAITING FOR ME TO LEARN ABOUT OR DIS-COVER! SO IN OTHER WORDS, SOMETHING MAGICAL THAT I CAN SHARE WITH EACH AND EVERY ONE OF YOU!

I'LL ADMIT, AT FIRST I WAS A BIT NERVOUS WHEN I LEARNED I'D BE SPEAKING HERE TODAY. BUT YOUR SMILING FACES LIT A FIRE IN ME THAT I WON'T LET GO OUT! I'LL LEARN TONS OF NEW THINGS AND BE SURE TO SHARE THEM ALL WITH YOU! BECAUSE BY THEN... I SHOULD HAVE AN ANSWER FOR EVERYTHING! THAT'S A PROMISE, SO DON'T YOU FORGET IT!

ENDING THINGS ON A PROMISE, EH? THAT'S A NICE TOUCH! IT'S A PRETTY BIG ONE THOUGH... YA THINK YOU'LL BE ABLE TO KEEP IT?

CONSIDERING I'VE SEEN YOU MAKE AND KEEP PROMISES FAR MORE AMBITIOUS, I DON'T SEE WHY NOT. BESIDES, I DID LEARN FROM THE BEST, AFTER ALL.

FSSS...

YOU'RE DARN RIGHT YA DID! NOW, LET'S ROLL! WE'VE GOT BUSINESS TO TAKE CARE OF.

MORE THAN MOST WOULD EVER DARE TO IMAGINE, DAVE WAS CERTAINLY RIGHT THAT WE NEEDED TO LEAVE.

THOUGH I WOULD'VE LOVED TO STAY HERE TO CHAT FOR JUST A LITTLE WHILE LONGER...

BUT THE TRUTH IS, THERE WAS A SEVERE SITUATION TO ATTEND TO, AND TIME WAS OF THE ESSENCE.

I DO WISH THAT I HAD SOME EXTRA TIME TO COME UP WITH A MORE HEART-FELT GOODBYE, THOUGH. IT WAS GOOD. I JUST FEEL LIKE IT COULD'VE BEEN A TINY BIT BETTER. BUT THE TRUTH IS, WE ONLY GET ONE SHOT AT THINGS SOMETIMES... FOR BETTER OR WORSE, I SUPPOSE.

THERE ARE TIMES AND PLACES TO HAVE REGRETS, BUT THIS ONE WASN'T EITHER OF THOSE. BECAUSE WHAT I WOULD GO THROUGH NEXT COULD ONLY BE SUMMARIZED AS A SERIES OF HECTIC EVENTS THAT WOULD CATAPULT ME IN THE DIRECTION OF MY GREATEST ADVENTURE YET. SO STICK AROUND, AND I'LL CATCH YOU ON THE FLIP SIDE!

CHAPTER 3, END.

113

ADVENTURER'S NOTES #3

WELP, I HOPE EVERYTHING'S MADE SENSE SO FAR. IT'S BEEN A LOT, FOR YOU AND ME BOTH. SO FEEL FREE TO TAKE A BREAK, KICK BACK WITH SOME FRIENDS, AND JUST RELAX FOR A BIT BEFORE WE MOVE ON AHEAD.

BUT I GET IT. NOT *EVERYONE* IS CAPABLE OF SETTLING DOWN, I SUPPOSE. CASE IN POINT, MY LITTLE "EXPERIMENTS" SPENT A FEW HOURS VIOLENTLY BRAWLING WITH EACH OTHER, WHILE THE REST OF US JUST SAT THERE AND WATCHED.

ONE OF THEM MADE SOME WEAPONS AND A SUIT OF ARMOR, AND ANOTHER FOUND A REALLY SMALL FOLDING CHAIR TO FIGHT WITH. NO IDEA WHERE FROM THOUGH, BUT I WAS STILL PRETTY IMPRESSED!

IT'S ALSO WORTH MENTIONING THAT I'M NOT REALLY SURE WHAT THEY'RE UP TO RIGHT NOW. THEY SORT OF RAN OFF INTO THE WOODS AND I HAVEN'T SEEN 'EM SINCE. I'M NOT WORRIED ABOUT IT THOUGH. I'M SURE THEY'LL POP UP AGAIN SOONER OR LATER.

WELL, DISREGARDING THAT... I'M GETTING A REALLY STRONG SIGNAL OVER IN THIS DIRECTION.

Grrr

IT FEELS THE SAME AS BEFORE, BUT ALMOST A BIT MORE INTENSE THIS TIME, FOR SOME REASON.

OH WAIT, I THINK I GOT IT! I CAN ACTUALLY SEE A BIG SPARK OF IT RIGHT OVER-

HERE.

OH...

YOU KNOW, IN RETROSPECT, YOU COULD'VE JUST TOLD ME HE WAS THERE INSTEAD OF LETTING ME MAKE A FOOL OF MYSELF, RIGHT?

OH, COME ON! WHERE'S THE FUN IN THAT?

YOU!!!

YEAH. ME.

WHAT'S IT TO YOU?

EVERYTHING.

HMMM...

WELL, THAT'S CONCERNING.

HEY, ALEX. YA MIND DOIN' ME A SOLID AND TAKIN' A COUPLE STEPS BACK?

I'D RATHER NOT GET BARBECUED TODAY. SO YEAH, SURE THING!

119

WELL... THAT WAS GRAVELY HUMILIATING.

BUT NO MATTER. THE SEARCH IS OVER. THIS IS THE ONE.

THOUGH HIS IDENTITY AS THE TRUE INCARNATION...

YET REMAINS UNPROVEN.

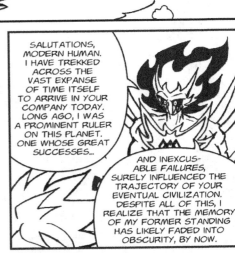

SALUTATIONS, MODERN HUMAN. I HAVE TREKKED ACROSS THE VAST EXPANSE OF TIME ITSELF TO ARRIVE IN YOUR COMPANY TODAY. LONG AGO, I WAS A PROMINENT RULER ON THIS PLANET. ONE WHOSE GREAT SUCCESSES...

AND INEXCUS-ABLE FAILURES, SURELY INFLUENCED THE TRAJECTORY OF YOUR EVENTUAL CIVILIZATION. DESPITE ALL OF THIS, I REALIZE THAT THE MEMORY OF MY FORMER STANDING HAS LIKELY FADED INTO OBSCURITY, BY NOW.

NEVERTHELESS, MY ACTIONS SPOKE FOR THEMSELVES. I AM SURE THAT MY DEEDS PROVIDED THE BASIS FOR MANY DESPICABLE TALES THAT YOUR PEOPLE HAVE FORGED OVER THE LAST SEVERAL MILLENNIA.

AND DESPITE THE MANY PSEUDONYMS I AM SURE WERE FABRICATED FOR ME IN THEM, I WILL REMIND YOU, HERE AND NOW, OF THE TREMENDOUS TITLE HELD BY THE MOST UNSTOPPABLE FORCE YOUR PLANET HAS EVER SEEN! MY TRUE NAME, IS-

UP 'TIL NOW, I'VE KEPT THIS ONE UNDER WRAPS, BUT IT'S NO DOUBT ONE OF MY FAVORITES.

I CAN DEMONST-RATE IT A BIT FURTHER IF YOU LIKE...

THOUGH YOU'LL NEED TO TAKE A FEW STEPS BACK AGAIN FOR ME, PLEASE.

SURE, NO PROB!

ALRIGHT! JUST TRY AND IGNORE THIS!!!

ALRIGHT! JUST TRY AND GET A LOAD OF THIS!

LIKE I SAID, HYPER-SPUN HALO IS ONE OF MY FAVORITES, BUT DO YA KNOW WHY? I'LL TELL YA!

IT'S 'CAUSE ONCE ONE'S ACTIVE, YOU CAN TRANSITION TO DIFFERENT SPELLS WITHOUT THE NEED FOR CONSCIOUS THOUGHT.

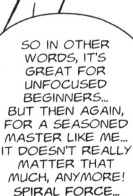

SO IN OTHER WORDS, IT'S GREAT FOR UNFOCUSED BEGINNERS... BUT THEN AGAIN, FOR A SEASONED MASTER LIKE ME... IT DOESN'T REALLY MATTER THAT MUCH, ANYMORE! SPIRAL FORCE...

123

CYCLONE CANNON

124

THOUGH BACK WHEN I FIRST STARTED, IT WAS PRETTY CONVENIENT.

BUT THAT WAS A REAL LONG TIME AGO. LET'S FOCUS ON THE HERE AND NOW.

HEY, ALEX! I HOPE YA DON'T PLAN ON LEAVING ME WITH ALL THE WORK ON THIS ONE! I'VE GOT A JOB FOR YA TO DO AND IT'S KINDA IMPORTANT.

TAKE THIS.

YOU'LL NEED IT FOR WHAT YOU HAVE TO DO.

IT'S ALL YOURS.

FINALLY!

THINK OF IT AS A BONUS.

BUT ALL OF THAT ASIDE, LET ME CUT TO THE CHASE.

THAT BONEHEAD OVER THERE MIGHT NOT KNOW HOW TO THROW A PUNCH, BUT HE'S NO PUSHOVER.

AND IF THINGS GET DICEY, I MIGHT NEED TO GO ALL OUT... WHETHER I LIKE IT OR NOT.

EVEN IF IT DOESN'T COME TO THAT, I'D HATE TO SEE ANY INNOCENT PEOPLE GET HURT 'CAUSE OF ALL THE COLLATERAL.

BUT LUCKY FOR THEM, THAT'S WHERE YOU COME IN!

HEY, YOU! YOUR NAME. IT'S *TEMBRIS* RIGHT?

GET UP!

Y-YOU KNOW ME?!

YEAH, OF COURSE! WHAT DO I LOOK LIKE, A SLOUCH?

THOUGH I AM PLEASED THAT SOMEONE KNOWS OF MY NAME, IT IS NOT THE REASON I HAVE SOUGHT OUT YOUR PRESENCE, MODERN WARRIOR.

I DO NOT KNOW THE MEANING OF THE WORD "SLOUCH", BUT I AM SURE YOU ARE NOT ONE OF THEM.

I HAVE COME IN SEARCH OF A REBORN RIVAL FROM MANY LIFETIMES AGO. AND I BELIEVE THAT YOU, THE MOST POWERFUL PERSON IN THIS TIME PERIOD, MAY BE JUST THE ONE I AM LOOKING FOR. SO LET US SPEAK NO FURTHER WITH OUR VOICES, BUT INSTEAD THROUGH THE LANGUAGE OF COMBAT. SHOW ME WHAT YOU CAN DO.

YOU KNOW, THAT'S GOOD TO HEAR. YOU WOULDN'T KNOW ABOUT ANY OF THIS, BUT ONE OF MY PET PEEVES IS HOW IN MOVIES OR TV SHOWS, THE HERO AND THE VILLAIN SPEND ALL THIS TIME TALKING BACK AND FORTH RIGHT BEFORE THE FIGHT STARTS. USUALLY JUST FOR EXPOSITION'S SAKE.

BECAUSE WHILE THEY'RE BUSY HURLIN' ONE-LINERS AT EACH OTHER.

OR WHILE ONE'S TELLIN' THE OTHER ONE ABOUT THEIR SECRET PAST, OR HOW TRAGIC THEIR BACKSTORY IS...

ALL EVERYBODY'S REALLY WISHIN' THEY COULD SAY TO THOSE TWO IDIOTS HALF THE TIME...

IS TO JUST CAN IT, AND GET ON WITH THE ACTION ALREADY!!!

BAM!

HE'S EVEN FASTER THAN BEFORE...

WSHHH!

?!

KSHH!

MACROBURST

135

PAIRED
WITH

PINPOINT
PUMMELING

CRASHH!!!

THE KEY DIFFERENCE BETWEEN YOUR POWER AND MINE, HOWEVER...

IS THAT THE NEED TO LIMIT MY WILL WITHIN THE CONFINES OF A SO-CALLED "SPELL"...

IS A WEAKNESS I OVERCAME, A VERY LONG TIME AGO!!!

DARKTALON

SLASH!!

NIGHTBLAZE

I'VE ALREADY SAID, I'M A SEASONED MASTER, NOT A BEGINNER. BUT WITH THAT EARLY HALLOWEEN MASK OVER YOUR EARS, YOU PROB- ABLY COULDN'T HEAR ME, EVEN IF YOU WANTED TO. STILL, MAN... IT SURE IS FUNNY.

FUNNY THAT YOU REALLY THINK YOU'RE THE ONLY ONE WHO OVERCAME THAT BARRIER, HUH? SORRY TO BREAK IT TO YA, BUT I ONLY SPEAK MY SPELLS ALOUD SOMETIMES JUST 'CAUSE IT'S A LONGSTANDING TRADITION. I DON'T ACTUALLY *NEED* TO SAY ANYTHING.

OH?

YEAH. BUT IF HOW YA DRESS IS ANY INDI- CATION...

IT'S PRETTY CLEAR THAT YOU DON'T KNOW A DARN THING ABOUT STYLE. SO, I DOUBT YOU'D UNDERSTAND.

142

ALRIGHT...

SO AFTER THAT CONFUSING SERIES OF EVENTS...

CRMBLE

OOPS!

I'M SURE MOST OF YOU OUT THERE MUST HAVE SOME, UH...

HAHA, GOTCHA!

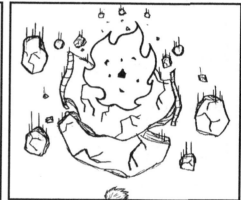

...WHAT?

BOOM!

BURNING QUESTIONS... THAT YOU'D PROBABLY LIKE THE ANSWERS TO.

PUN: FULLY INTENDED.

YO!

POOF!

FOR STARTERS, I'D ALREADY BEGUN DOING EXACTLY WHAT DAVE SAID TO DO. BEGINNING WITH EVERYONE AT THE AUDITORIUM, I LAUNCHED A FULL-SCALE EVACUATION OF THE ENTIRE CITY.

BUT HONESTLY, THAT'S PRETTY LACKLUSTER COMPARED TO EVERYTHING ELSE GOING ON TODAY.

ASIDE FROM THAT, YOU MIGHT BE WONDERING SOMETHING LIKE...

"SINCE WHEN DOES DAVE HAVE SUPERPOWERS AND WHY'S HE FIGHTING THAT TEMBRIS GUY?!"

THE ANSWERS TO BOTH GO HAND-IN-HAND, ACTUALLY.

149

I DON'T HAVE ANY POWERS. ER, WELL... NOT IN THIS LIFE, YET.

BUT THEN AGAIN, NEITHER DO ANY OTHER HUMANS, THESE DAYS.

AT LEAST... NOT QUITE LIKE DAVE'S, I SUPPOSE.

BUT I'M GETTING AHEAD OF MYSELF.

AS FOR TEMBRIS, WELL, LUCKILY HE HELPS ME PIVOT ONTO MY NEXT POINT. WHAT A GUY!

IT'S PROBABLY GETTING REPETITIVE BY NOW, SO I'LL STOP BEING SO CRYPTIC ABOUT IT. LONG AGO, THE REASON WHY ANCIENT EARTH WAS SO DIFFERENT FROM HOW IT IS TODAY...

WAS DUE TO THE PRESENCE OF AN INCREDIBLY RARE AND POWERFUL SUBSTANCE CALLED *AURUM*. WITH IT'S INFINITE USES THAT WENT BEYOND PRIMITIVE UNDERSTANDING...

AURUM GAVE RISE TO MANY MIRACLES THAT HELPED HUMANITY LEARN TO BELIEVE IN OURSELVES. BACK IN AN AGE WHEN THE FUTURE LOOKED BRIGHT, AND EVERY DREAM WE HAD FELT LIKELY TO COME TRUE.

PLAN B: BEAT TEMBRIS, TAKE BACK ALL THE AURUM, AND RESTORE THIS WORLD'S LONG-LOST POTENTIAL.

BUT DESPERATELY, WE GAVE UP MOST OF IT JUST TO STUFF TEMBRIS IN A POT, WHICH SUBSE-QUENTLY STUNTED OUR GROWTH FOR COUNTLESS GENERATIONS... BUT THAT WAS PLAN A! ONTO PLAN B.

POOF!

SEEMS EASY ENOUGH, RIGHT? YEAH. IF ONLY THINGS ALWAYS WORKED OUT EXACTLY THE WAY YOU PLANNED THEM TO.

151

CHAPTER 4, END.

ADVENTURER'S NOTES #4

FINALLY! THE NORTHSTAR IS MINE, AND I COULDN'T BE HAPPIER! THIS LITTLE GADGET IS REALLY SOMETHING ELSE, SO WHOEVER MADE IT MUST'VE BEEN ONE HECK OF A GENIUS!

FAIR TO SAY, IT'S ONLY BEEN MINE FOR A SHORT TIME, BUT I THINK I'VE REALLY GOTTEN THE HANG OF IT! I EVEN HAVE A PRETTY SOLID IDEA OF HOW IT FUNCTIONS TOO, IF YOU'RE INTERESTED IN HEARING ABOUT IT.

THE NORTHSTAR'S TELEPORTATION ABILITIES COME BY WAY OF THE METHOD IT USES TO CONTROL AND MANIPULATE DISTANCES IN SPACE.

TO BRING THE USER TO THE LOCATION OF THEIR CHOOSING, THE NORTHSTAR SHORTENS THE DISTANCE IN FRONT OF THE USER, AND EXPANDS THE DISTANCE BEHIND THEM IN ONE RAPID SURGE OF INSTANTANEOUS MOVEMENT.

BUT NOT SO FAST! THESE AWESOME SPACE-WARPING AND TELEPORTATIONAL ABILITIES CAN ONLY BE USED IF THE NORTHSTAR HAS ENOUGH ENERGY INSIDE OF IT TO SERVE AS A POWER SOURCE. OTHERWISE, IT'S JUST AN ORDINARY DISK.

AND ONE MORE THING!

THE NORTHSTAR GENERATES AND CLOAKS ITS USERS IN A SPECIAL AURA. IT MAKES YOU BECOME TEMPORARILY INTANGIBLE, SO YOU CAN PASS THROUGH SOLID OBJECTS WHILE IN THE PROCESS OF TELEPORTING.

ALSO, THE IMMENSE AMOUNT OF ENERGY USED DURING TELEPORTATION CREATES LITTLE PUFFS OF STEAM TOO! IT'S NOT MUCH, BUT IT'S A PRETTY NICE AESTHETIC THAT I'VE ALWAYS THOUGHT WAS COOL!

WHAT'S THE MATTER? STARTIN' TO LOSE YOUR NERVE?

GRRR!!

CHAPTER 5: OPERATION EVACUATION

HARDLY. UP UNTIL NOW, YOU'VE ONLY WITNESSED A FRACTION OF WHAT MY REVIVED STATE IS TRULY CAPABLE OF.

INSTEAD, I THINK YOU WILL BE THE ONE "LOSING YOUR NERVE" IF I CHOOSE TO EXCEED BEYOND ITS CURRENT LIMITATIONS.

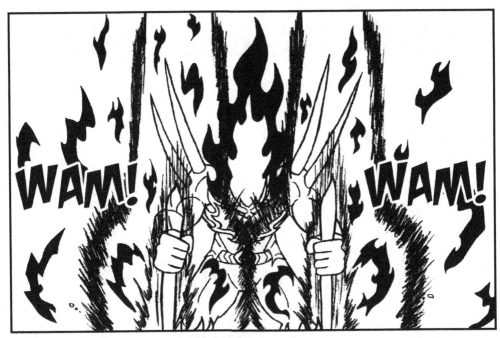

WAM! WAM!

BESIDES! WHY WOULD I EXERT UNNECESSARY EFFORT WHEN I HAVE MINIONS WHO COULD DO IT FOR ME?!

MINIONS, EH? AW MAN, THIS SHOULD BE INTERESTING.

155

YES. I WILL HAVE YOU KNOW, I AM EXCEEDINGLY PROUD OF THESE LITTLE PETS OF MINE.

THEY SHARE A SORT OF... LOYAL FORM OF AGGRESSION THAT I AM INDEED QUITE FOND OF.

AND THE FACT THAT IT NEARLY GUARANTEES THE DEMISE FOR WHOEVER FIRST MEETS A BASILISK'S GAZE...

ONLY MAKES MY ADMIRATION FOR THEM ALL THE MORE OBVIOUS. SO, TRY TO RUN. TRY TO HIDE. NONE OF IT MATTERS.

MY BASILISKS WON'T STOP ATTACKING UNTIL THEIR PREY'S LIFE IS TERMINATED.

THE ONLY WAY TO SURVIVE IS BY DESTROYING THEM BOTH.

DO THAT, AND YOU WILL HAVE PROVEN YOURSELF WORTHY OF WITNESSING MY TRUE POWER.

CRASH! BOOM!

ALRIGHT.

ONE LAST GROUP, AND THAT'LL WRAP THINGS UP.

159

SORRY I'M LATE, BUT WE REALLY NEED TO GET OUT OF HERE.

I NEED YOU TO COME WITH ME RIGHT A-

WAY...

WHAT THE HECK ARE YOU DOING STUFFING YOUR FACE AT A TIME LIKE THIS?!?!

WHY? IS SOMETHING WRONG?

YUM!

WHAT DO YOU MEAN?! THERE ARE MURDEROUS SNAKES OUTSIDE!!

OF COURSE SOMETHING'S WRONG!!!

OH, I KNOW. I LOST THEM EVACUATING OVER 1.3 MILLION PEOPLE, ALONG WITH ALL OF THEIR PETS AGO.

SORRY FOR YOUR INCON- VENIENCE.

PHEW... FINALLY!

THAT'S EVERY- ONE.

ME

OR, WELL... AT LEAST I *THINK* THAT'S EVERYONE.

163

IT WAS AN UNREWARDING TASK. ONE THAT WAS OFTEN MET WITH... UNNECESSARY GLIMPSES INTO PEOPLE'S PERSONAL LIVES.

OUR BABY HASN'T SLEPT IN 3 DAYS, ANTHONY!

OKAY, WELL WHAT DO YOU WANT ME TO DO ABOUT IT?!

I WANT YOU TO STOP MESSING AROUND AND HELP ME, DARN IT!

UM... EXCUSE ME?

HABA! HABA!

BUT AGAINST ALL ODDS...

AGAINST ALL DANGERS...

AND AGAINST ALL FEELINGS OF REPULSION AND DOUBT, I PERSISTED.

HAROLD, IS THAT YOU?

GAH!

AND IN THE END, I'D MANAGED TO GET EVERYONE TO SAFETY BY MOVING THEM TO A LARGE CLEARING ON THE OUTSKIRTS OF THE CITY. THE MISSION WAS COMPLETE. THE DAY FELT WON. BUT AT WHAT COST?...

THE COST OF ALL MY PATIENCE AND A MOMENTARY LOSS OF SANITY! THAT'S WHAT!!!

165

YEAH, WELL ADVENTURE WAITS FOR NO ONE. HAHA.

GASP! ◇

WAIT A SEC, YOU'RE ALEX FROM SPIRIT OF ADVENTURE, RIGHT?

I THOUGHT IT WAS YOU! BUT YOU WERE HAVING A BREAK-DOWN EARLIER, SO I DIDN'T ASK.

HAHA, YEAH. TODAY'S BEEN PRETTY ROUGH. DON'T WORRY THOUGH, BREAKDOWN'S OVER.

BUT YUP, YOU GUESSED IT! THAT'S ME! IT'S SO COOL THAT YOU RECOGNIZED ME FROM SOA, IT REALLY MEANS A LOT!

(SOA: SPIRIT OF ADVENTURE)

I GUESS THAT MEANS YOU'RE A FAN OF THE SHOW THEN, RIGHT?

OH ALEX. YOU THINK I'M JUST A "FAN"? PLEASE...

I'D RATHER YOU THINK OF ME MORE AS A SEASONED CONNOISSEUR WHO VALUES YOUR SERIES' HIGH LEVEL OF ENTERTAINMENT, BEYOND THE TYPICAL NORM.

I'VE BEEN WATCHING SPIRIT OF ADVENTURE FOR OVER HALF MY LIFE! AND TRUST ME, WHEN I FIRST DISCOVERED IT, IT WAS LIFE-CHANGING!

I MEAN, I AM ONLY 8. SO, I KNOW IT'S NOT A WHOLE LOTTA LIFE TO CHANGE... BUT THAT DOESN'T MATTER!

OH, I GET IT. YOU'RE LIKE A "SUPER FAN" THEN, HUH? HAHA...

I THINK THE WAY YOU GUYS BATTLE CRAZY MONSTERS AND PUT BAD GUYS IN THEIR PLACE IS AS GOOD AS IT GETS! PLUS, I'VE LITERALLY NEVER MISSED AN EPISODE SINCE THE DAY YOU TOOK OVER! YOU'RE MY INSPIRATION!

...

HEY, YOU WANNA HELP ME WITH A MISSION?

HECK YEAH!

SERIOUSLY?! AWESOME! YOU'RE THE BEST!

TELL ME SOMETHIN' I DON'T KNOW, HON.

ALRIGHT! THIS THING HERE IS CALLED THE NORTHSTAR. I NEVER REALLY TALKED ABOUT IT DURING ANY SOA EPISODES, BUT IT BASICALLY LETS ME TELEPORT TO ANY LOCATION THAT I CAN IMAGINE.

LONG STORY SHORT, I'VE STILL GOT A FRIEND BACK THERE WHO COULD REALLY USE IT'S POWER SHOULD THINGS GET TOO FAR OUT OF HAND.

167

AH, I SEE. SO LEMME GUESS...

YOU'RE SHORT ON TIME, AND YOU NEED SOMEONE TO GET ALL OF THESE PEOPLE THAT YOU'VE ROUNDED UP EVEN FURTHER AWAY FROM ALL OF THIS CHAOS... WHILE YOU GO AND HELP OUT YOUR FRIEND. IS THAT RIGHT?

WOW! YEAH, YOU GOT IT! THAT ABOUT SUMS IT UP!

YOU REALLY DO KNOW YOUR STUFF. I'M IMPRESSED!

HEHE! OF COURSE YOU ARE! YOU SAID I'M THE BEST, AND IT'S FOR GOOD REASON!

MAYBE IT'S 'CAUSE YOU SENSED MY AURA OF UNMATCHED CAPABLENESS! OR MAYBE IT'S 'CAUSE YOU KNEW THAT MY PERSUASION SKILLS AND NATURAL CHARMS WERE OF THE UTMOST CALIBER! OR MAYBE-

WELL... ACTUALLY, IT'S ONLY 'CAUSE NOBODY ELSE EVER OFFERED TO HELP ME WITH ANY OF THIS.

DOESN'T MATTER! I'M STILL THE BEST!

OH, HUSH CYRUS!

MEOW...

(YEAH. BY DEFAULT.)

YOU KNOW, I'M NOT SURE WHAT THAT LITTLE GUY'S SAYING ABOUT YOU OVER THERE, BUT I'M SURE IT'S SOMETHING GREAT.

(FINE. I SNOOZE INSTEAD.)

RAWR...

I GUESS HIS NAME MUST BE CYRUS, RIGHT? BUT NOW THAT I THINK ABOUT IT...

I NEVER CAUGHT YOURS, DID I? WHAT'S YOUR NAME, KID?

168

169

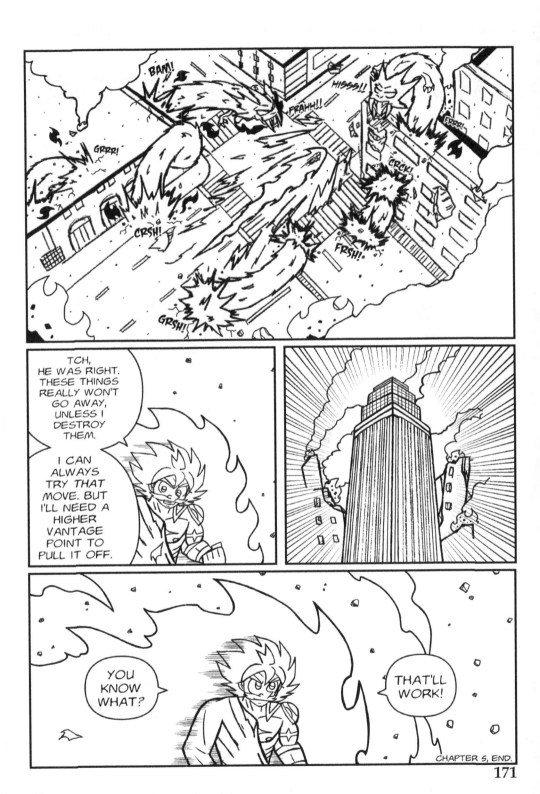

TCH, HE WAS RIGHT. THESE THINGS REALLY WON'T GO AWAY, UNLESS I DESTROY THEM.

I CAN ALWAYS TRY *THAT* MOVE. BUT I'LL NEED A HIGHER VANTAGE POINT TO PULL IT OFF.

YOU KNOW WHAT?

THAT'LL WORK!

CHAPTER 5, END.

171

Adventurer's Notes #5

SUCCESS! EVACUATION COMPLETE! BUT WE CAN'T FORGET ABOUT ALL OF OUR OTHER NON-HUMAN FRIENDS, RIGHT? 'CAUSE AFTER ALL, IN THE EVENT OF AN EMERGENCY, BIG OR SMALL, WE LEAVE NOBODY BEHIND!

RIGHT HERE, WE'VE GOT SOME OF OUR PARK-DWELLERS. BIRDS, DUCKS, RACCOONS, CHIPMUNKS, SQUIRRELS, AND OTHER CRITTERS LIKE THAT.

THEN OVER HERE, WE'VE GOT OUR MORE AQUATIC AND SEMI-AQUATIC BUDDIES WHO NEEDED SAVING. LOBSTERS, CRABS, FISH, SHARKS, DOLPHINS, STINGRAYS, EELS, FROGS, MANATEES, AND PRETTY MUCH ANY OTHER KIND OF CREATURE YOU'D FIND IN A PERSONAL OR COMMERCIAL AQUARIUM. OF COURSE, THAT'S A LOT TO DRAW. SO, HERE'S ME WITH JUST THE LOBSTERS. I HOPE THAT'LL SUFFICE!

THEN, LAST BUT NOT LEAST, WE'VE GOT OUR BEASTS KEPT IN ZOOS. AT FIRST, THEY WEREN'T BIG FANS OF ME POPPING IN UNEXPECTEDLY. BUT THEY WARMED UP LATER AFTER I BROUGHT THEM TO A WILDLIFE SANCTUARY. I'M SURE THEY'LL BE MUCH HAPPIER THERE ANYWAY.

OF COURSE, HANDLING A LARGE-SCALE RELOCATION ON SUCH SHORT NOTICE SURE ISN'T EASY. BUT IN THE END, I PULLED IT OFF. THAT IN ITSELF WAS ONE HECK OF A TASK, BUT IT WAS THE LEAST I COULD DO. IN FACT, WHEN YOU TAKE AWAY ALL OF THE BRUISES AND SOME OF THE TATTERED CLOTHES, I GOTTA ADMIT, IT WAS PRETTY DARN FUN!

CHAPTER 6:
WILL OF THE
DRAGON

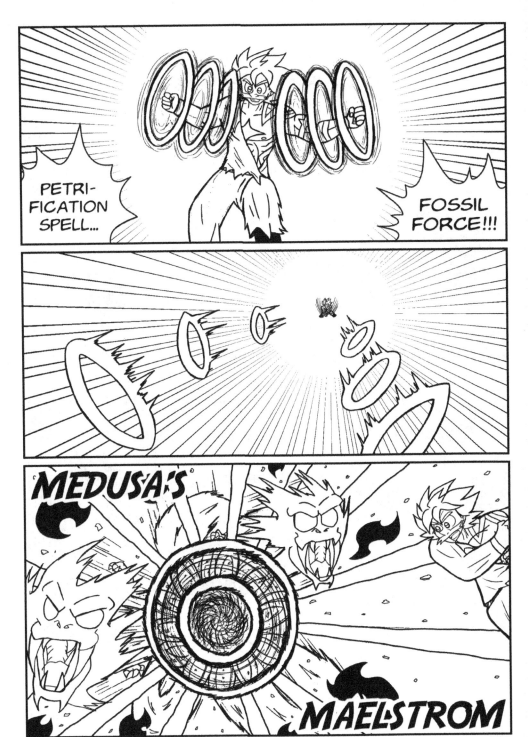

BRAVO, MODERN MAN. BRAVO. TURNING THE BASILISKS INTO STONE...

WHAT AN INCREDIBLE IDEA! YOU ARE INDEED WORTHY.

177

YEAH, YEAH. SPARE ME THE COMPLIMENTS AND SHOW ME THAT *TRUE* POWER OR WHATEVER YOU WERE TALKIN' ABOUT EARLIER.

AND MAKE IT SNAPPY! YOU'RE KEEPIN' THIS GEEZER HERE IN SUSPENSE, AND I'D RATHER NOT WAIT ALL DAY FOR SOMETHIN' COOL TO HAPPEN.

OH, I ASSURE YOU. THE WAIT IS OVER.

I TOLD YOU BEFORE. THE TRUE POWER OF MY REVIVED STATE...

IS NOT A REALM I CAN FULLY INHABIT WITHOUT EXCEEDING BEYOND ITS CURRENT LIMITATIONS.

BUT MY WORDS ARE ABSOLUTE. AND I RETRACT NOTHING. BESIDES, YOU'VE EARNED THIS PRIVELEGE.

THE PRIVELEGE TO MEET YOUR END THROUGH THE EMBODIEMENT OF SUFFERING ITSELF!!! METABLAZE! TARTAREAN TRANSFORMATION!! *INCINEBRIS!!!*

SO YOUR ULTIMATE MOVE'S JUST A BIGGER FIREBALL, HUH? THAT'S PRETTY DISAPPOINTING.

YOU SHOULD'VE LEARNED YOUR LESSON BY NOW. MOVES LIKE THAT ARE JUST TOO EASY TO COUNTER. ESPECIALLY FOR ME.

OH, I'M ALREADY AWARE OF YOUR APTITUDE FOR REPELLING ATTACKS OF THIS VARIETY.

HOWEVER... THIS ATTACK IS FAR MORE DANGEROUS THAN THE ONE YOU'D FACED LAST TIME.

SO FOR YOUR SAKE, I HOPE YOU CAN COUNTER THIS! BECAUSE IF YOU DON'T...

THEN EVERYTHING BEFORE YOU WILL BE REDUCED TO ASHES!!!

BECAUSE FACING DOWN DANGER IS JUST WHAT I DO.

BINDING SPELL...

ASTRAL FORCE!

184

187

188

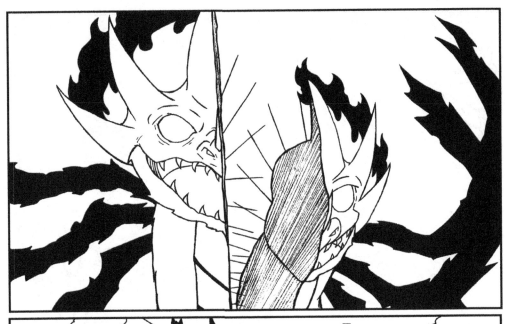

GRAAA AAGH!!

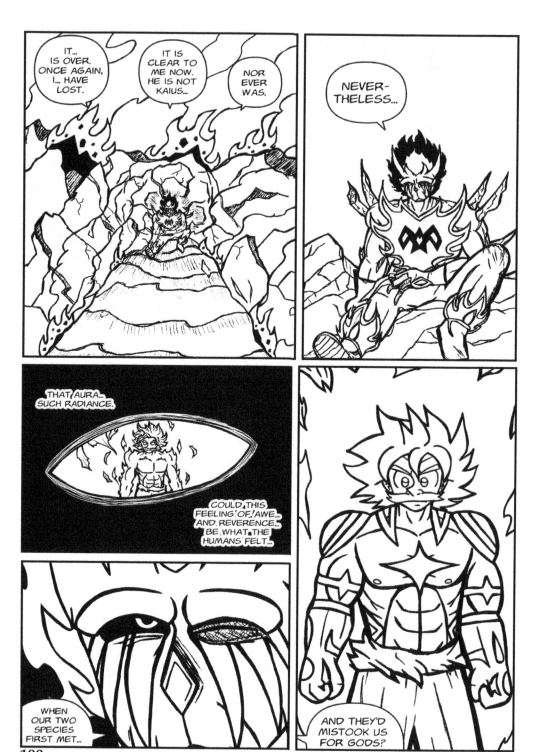

190

I'VE SEEN YOUR KIND FIGHT FOR... MANY REASONS.

BE THEM POWER, WEALTH, VENGEANCE, RECOGNITION, AND EVEN LOVE... AMONG OTHER THINGS.

AND ASIDE FROM A SELECT FEW... I HAVE NEVER MET SOMEONE AS GREAT A WARRIOR AS YOU.

SO TELL ME, HUMAN... WHO ARE YOU? WHAT DO YOU FIGHT FOR?

AND WHAT DROVE YOU... TO BECOME THIS STRONG?

MY NAME IS DAVID NORTHSTAR.

I BECAME AS STRONG AS I AM TODAY TO HONOR SOME PEOPLE I REALLY LOOKED UP TO. THAT WAY I COULD AT LEAST KEEP THEIR MEMORY ALIVE SOMEHOW.

YOU ALTERED THE FUTURE, THEN STOLE IT FROM THOSE WHO JUST WANTED TO MAKE OUR LIVES BETTER.

I BUILT THIS POWER SOLELY TO DEFEAT YOU. THAT WAY I COULD BRING THEM ALL BACK. IT DOESN'T GET ANY MORE COMPLICATED THAN THAT.

JUST LIKE THIS RUINED CITY, YOU LEFT THE WORLD IN SHAMBLES.

HEHEHE. YOU MUST BE REFERRING TO A SPECIFIC SET OF FOOLS I ONCE KNEW...

I'M SURE THEY WOULD BE HUMBLED TO KNOW THAT THEY INSPIRED SUCH GREATNESS.

IT'S A SHAME THEY COULDN'T BE HERE TO MEET YOU PERSONALLY.

IT'S UNFORTUNATE, BUT FOR THE UNEVOLVED, AURUM DEPLETION ALWAYS RESULTS IN A DISGRACEFUL DEMISE. HAHAHA...

192

AURA OF ANNIHILATION

ARAGH!!! WHAT ARE YOU DOING?!!

OH, THAT'S SIMPLE. YA SEE, A REALLY OLD FRIEND OF MINE GAVE ME THIS IDEA. BUT HIS EXPLANATION WAS A BIT TOO LONG-WINDED, WITH HIM BEING A PHYSICIST AND ALL.

BASICALLY, I'M USING MY RIGHT SIDE'S POWER TO HOLD YOU IN PLACE, AND MY LEFT SIDE'S POWER TO COMPLETELY DESTROY YOUR BODY... THUS RELEASING ALL OF THE AURUM YOU STOLE. IT'S THAT SIMPLE.

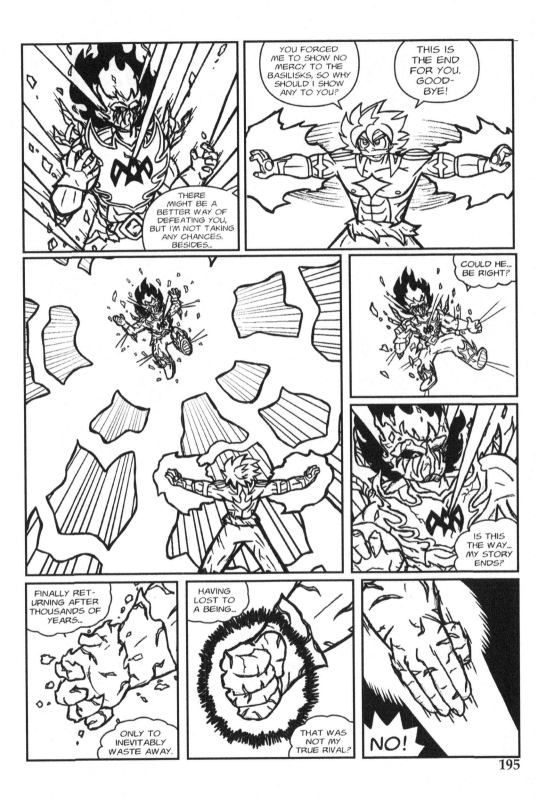

195

I NEVER IMAGINED I WOULD BE ABLE TO USE THIS POWER AGAINST ONE OF YOUR KIND, AS I'D NEVER BELIEVED IT WOULD AMOUNT TO ANYTHING.

HOWEVER... IT APPEARS AS THOUGH YOU ARE MORE LIKE MY PEOPLE THAN YOU MAY YET REALIZE... WHAT... AN ASTOUNDING DISCOVERY!

SIMPLY PUT, I POSSESS THE UNIQUE ABILITY TO REPLICATE THE ATTACKS OF OTHERS, TO WHICH I CAN THEN ADD TO MY OWN ARSENAL, SO AS LONG AS I RECEIVE SUFFICIENT DAMAGE FROM THE ORIGINAL ATTACKER IN THE FIRST PLACE.

THIS ABILITY ONLY FUNCTIONS WELL AGAINST THOSE OF MY OWN KIND. SO IT WOULD APPEAR AS THOUGH YOU HAVE A RATHER... INTERESTING ANCESTRY. HOW CONVENIENT!

SHHHHHHHH!!!

197

THEN AGAIN...

YOU COULD HAVE ALWAYS GOTTEN YOUR PROPORTIONS OFF.

AND WITHOUT ANY GUIDANCE, THAT WOULD NOT SURPRISE ME...

BUT WITH ENERGY THIS PURE, THERE IS NO MISTAKING IT. YOU CERTAINLY ARE A DESCENDANT OF AT LEAST ONE MY PEOPLE.

THE QUESTION IS... WHO THOUGH? BUT I SUPPOSE IT TRULY DOES NOT MATTER.

TO THINK THAT MYTHOI GENETICS PERSISTED DORMANTLY IN YOUR SPECIES FOR THIS LONG... REMARKABLE!!!

BUT NEVERTHELESS...

I CAN NOT HAVE YOU INTERFERING WITH ANY OF MY FURTHER PLANS.

SO, THIS IS THE END FOR YOU. GOODBYE.

ADVENTURER'S NOTES #6

AN OFTEN UNSTATED FACT ABOUT ALMOST ANY SUPER-POWERED FIGHT IS THAT NO MATTER HOW STRONG AN ATTACK MAY BE, THERE'S ALWAYS SOME WAY OUT THERE TO DEFEND YOURSELF AGAINST IT. AND AURUM-BASED POWERS ARE REALLY NO DIFFERENT! IN THE CASE OF SPELLS, WHERE ONE'S INTENT IS SPOKEN INTO BEING, AS WELL AS OTHER MORE ADVANCED REALITY-WARPING TECHNIQUES THAT BYPASS THAT REQUIREMENT, IT'S POSSIBLE TO NULLIFY AN ATTACK'S EFFECT(S) THROUGH THE USE OF VARIOUS METHODS.

AND TRUTH BE TOLD, THE FIRST ONE OF THESE METHODS IS PRETTY STRAIGHTFORWARD! IT SIMPLY INVOLVES USING BRUTE FORCE TO PHYSICALLY TANK/ENDURE THE PROPORTIONAL AMOUNT OF DAMAGE CAUSED BY AN ATTACK. IF ONE'S BODY POSSESSES A SUFFICIENT LEVEL OF OVERALL RESILIENCE, THEY CAN BLOCK HITS AND EFFECTIVELY DEFEND AGAINST ATTACKS OF A CERTAIN VARIETY AND STRENGTH LEVEL. HOWEVER, THIS METHOD OF DEFENSE IS LIMITED SOLELY TO SPELLS AND TECHNIQUES THAT CAUSE DAMAGE DIRECTLY, AND IS NOT EFFICIENT AT RESISTING THOSE THAT SUPPLY ADDITIONAL EFFECTS.

SUCH ADDITIONAL EFFECTS CAN BE NEGATED BY USING ANOTHER METHOD. THIS ONE INVOLVES USING ONE'S OWN POWER TO CREATE A WELL-TIMED COUNTER MEASURE. BY NOW, WE'RE ALREADY FAMILIAR WITH SOME EXAMPLES OF THESE, SUCH AS COUNTER SPELLS AND BINDING SPELLS. BUT MANY OTHER ALTERNATIVE MEASURES CAN BE USED TO HELP TURN THE TIDE IN THE MIDST OF A HEATED BATTLE. ALTERNATIVES INCLUDE USING OFFENSE IN THE FORM OF DEFENSE. ATTACKS UTILIZED IN A CREATIVE MANNER HAVE THE POTENTIAL TO SERVE AS EXCELLENT BARRIERS. GENERALLY SPEAKING, THE STRENGTH OF THE COUNTER ATTACK SHOULD AT LEAST MATCH OR SURPASS THAT OF THE OPPOSITION IN ORDER TO SERVE AS AN OPTIMAL DEFENSE.

HOWEVER, SINCE THE MANIPULATION OF AURUM TO ALTER REALITY IS A POWER FORTIFIED BY ONE'S PUREST INTENTIONS AND OVERALL WILL, THERE ARE RARE INSTANCES WHERE STRENGTH ALONE DOES NOT GUARANTEE THE OUTCOME ONE WOULD USUALLY EXPECT. IF EVEN FOR ONE BRIEF MOMENT, THE WILLPOWER OF ONE USER/GROUP OF USERS SEVERELY OVERPOWERS THAT OF ANOTHER, THE EFFECTS OF AN OPPOSING ATTACK CAN BE NULLIFIED AND OVERCOME, EVEN IF THE STRONGER-WILLED USER(S) IS/ARE AT AN EXTREME STRENGTH DISADVANTAGE.

CHAPTER 7:
HERO OF THE
NORTHSTAR

BRRRRRRR!!!

THAT DAUNTLESS GAZE...

SEEMED AWFULLY FAMILIAR.

203

206

SPRINGFIELD, PA, USA.

5:47 PM

YEAH... I'M ALRIGHT... I'M NOT REALLY SURE, BUT I'LL WAIT AND SEE...

MHM... THAT'S GOOD TO HEAR.

CREAK...

YEAH... I'LL STAY SAFE... LOVE YOU TOO, MOM.

TO REASSURE HER THAT I'D STAY SAFE.

ALEX... YOU CAN COME IN NOW.

THE GRAVITY OF THE SITUATION FULLY STRUCK, NOT LONG AFTER WE ESCAPED. WITH AN ENTIRE CITY UP IN FLAMES, AND A TYRANNICAL MANIAC ON THE LOOSE, THE WORLD WAS SHAPING UP TO BE AN EVEN MORE UNCERTAIN PLACE THAN IT ALREADY WAS. SO, I DID WHAT ANY CONCERNED PERSON WOULD DO AT A TIME LIKE THIS... I CALLED MY MOM.

THOUGH TO BE FULLY HONEST, I WASN'T SURE WHAT THE WORD "SAFE" TRULY MEANT ANYMORE.

THIS IS MY AUNT SANDRA, BY THE WAY. SHE'S THE CHIEF SURGEON AT THIS HOSPITAL...

AND ALSO HAPPENS TO BE BOTH THE BEST DOCTOR, AND THE BEST PERSON, THAT I KNOW.

OUT OF ESSENTIALLY EVERYBODY, SHE'S MY ONLY FAMILY MEMBER WHO'S SEEN FIRST-HAND JUST HOW DANGEROUS THE LIFE OF AN AEON FORCE MEMBER CAN TRULY BE...

SO, SHE'S THE ONE THAT I TRUST MOST TO COME TO WHENEVER A MISSION ENDS POORLY.

EH... WHAT'S UP DOC?

WAH?!

BRK!

SANDRA AND I HAVE BEEN CLOSE FOR AS LONG AS I CAN REMEMBER.

SANDRA: AGE 10

HE LOOKS LIKE AN "ALEX" TO ME!

ME: AGE 0

SHE WAS ONE OF THE FIRST PEOPLE I MET AND ALSO THE SAME ONE WHO NAMED ME, NOT LONG AFTER.

SINCE I'M THE OLDEST SIBLING IN MY IMMEDIATE FAMILY, AUNT SANDRA IS THE CLOSEST PERSON I'VE HAD IN MY LIFE TO AN OLDER SISTER...

SO, I'VE ALWAYS REALLY LOOKED UP TO HER.

BACK IN MY EARLY DAYS DOING THIS STUFF, I USED TO GET BEAT UP A LOT. AS YOU WOULD IMAGINE, IT WASN'T A VERY FUN TIME FOR ME.

OOF!

(NO SUPPLY BELT. WHAT A NOOB!)

YOU LOSE.

GIVE UP!

BUT SANDRA IS ONE OF THE FEW PEOPLE THAT DAVE IS ACTUALLY AFRAID OF...

SO WHENEVER I GOT INJURED, I AT LEAST HAD SOMETHING TO LOOK FORWARD TO.

I DON'T CARE IF YOU WERE BUSY FIGHTING VAMPIRES! THERE IS NO EXCUSE FOR HIM TO COME BACK WOUNDED ALL THE TIME!

JUST TEACH HIM HOW TO KICK THE BAD GUYS' BUTTS OR ELSE I'LL KICK YOURS, GOT IT?!

OK. YOU WIN. I GIVE UP.

ALTHOUGH, USUALLY I WAS THE ONE BARELY CLINGING TO LIFE WHENEVER WE WOULD VISIT...

SO, I WASN'T REALLY SURE HOW TO REACT NOW THAT THE ROLES HAD BEEN REVERSED.

ALRIGHT DOC, GIVE IT TO ME STRAIGHT... HOW BAD IS IT?

WELL, ASIDE FROM SOME BLOOD LOSS AND A FEW BROKEN BONES, NOT THAT BAD ACTUALLY.

THERE ARE STILL SOME OTHER COMPLICATIONS, BUT FROM A PHYSICAL STAND-POINT, HE'S DOING WELL.

SERIOUSLY? THAT'S GREAT TO HEAR! THANK YOU SO MUCH!

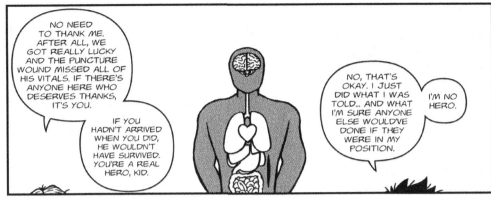

211

AN ALPHA-GLYPH?

I'M SORRY, WHAT?

AN ALPHA-GLYPH...

OH?

IT'S A PICTOGRAPHIC SYMBOL THAT AN ANCIENT WRITING SYSTEM CONSISTS OF.

ALSO CALLED ALPHAGLYPHICS WHEN USED TOGETHER, THESE SYMBOLS EVEN PREDATE CUNEIFORM USED IN EARLY MESOPOTAMIA.

THEY'RE FAIRLY COMMON TO FIND IN R.O.O.T. SITES AROUND THE WORLD. UN-FORTUNATELY, DAVE IS THE ONLY PERSON THAT I KNOW OF WHO'S CAPABLE OF DECIPHERING THEM.

I TRIED LEARNING ONCE FROM SOME VILLAGERS I'D BECOME FRIENDS WITH...

HEY, DO YOU KNOW WHAT THIS MEANS?

NAH BRO! IT'S JUST DECOR-ATION!

PFFFT!

OH...

BUT AS IT TURNS OUT, THEY DON'T REALLY KNOW WHAT THEY MEAN EITHER.

NOT LONG AFTER WE CLEANED AND SEALED THE WOUND...

DID SOMETHING VERY SINISTER BEGIN TO TAKE SHAPE.

FOR SOME, IT WAS A LOT TO PROCESS AT FIRST. BUT WHEN THE SPARKS FINALLY DID DIE DOWN...

THAT AWFUL SYMBOL HAD FORMED TO TAKE THEIR PLACE.

AND DESPITE BEING IN GOOD PHYSICAL CONDITION, HE HASN'T WOKEN UP SINCE.

WHATEVER THAT FIRE GUY DID TO HIM IS ANYONE'S GUESS...

BUT IF I DIDN'T KNOW ANY BETTER, I'D THINK HE WAS THE VICTIM OF SOME KIND OF... CURSE OR SOMETHING.

HE TOLD ME BEFORE THAT I SHOULD FOLLOW THE SYMBOLS...

AND TO FOLLOW MY HEART.

HE TOLD ME TO GO BACK TO THE PLACE WHERE IT ALL BEGAN.

I DOUBT THAT THE SYMBOL HE WAS REFERRING TO WAS THIS "CURSED" ONE, HOWEVER.

BUT MAYBE... JUST MAYBE... IF I GO BACK TO THAT PLACE...

THEN I JUST MIGHT FIGURE OUT HOW TO GET RID OF THAT THING.

THERE YOU GO AGAIN! OFF TO THE RACES FOR SOMEONE IN NEED, HUH?

AND YET YOU STILL REFUSE TO CALL YOURSELF A HERO.

PROMISE ME YOU WON'T PUSH YOURSELF TOO HARD THOUGH, OKAY?

YOU KNOW, I'VE ALWAYS LOVED GIFTS. SURE, I'M USUALLY NOT THE ONE POSITIONED ON THE RECEIVING END OF THE GIFT-GIVING SPECTRUM... BUT WHEN I AM, IT SURE DOES FEEL NICE!

I'VE NEVER STOPPED TO QUESTION WHY, BUT FOR ME, THERE'S A CERTAIN FAMILIARITY TO IT...

SOMETHING ABOUT IT JUST... REMINDS ME OF SOMEONE, PERHAPS FROM ANOTHER LIFE.

BUT MAYBE I'M JUST AN OLD SOUL WHO LIKES TO RAMBLE. I'M NOT REALLY SURE.

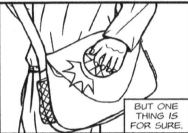

BUT ONE THING IS FOR SURE.

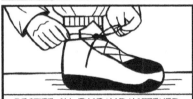

DESPITE ALL THAT HAD HAPPENED, AND HOW HOPELESS THINGS MIGHT'VE LOOKED, FOR ONE SHINING MOMENT...

I WAS TRULY EXCITED.

217

BUT THAT DIDN'T MEAN I COULD CARRY ON WITHOUT BEARING A HEFTY BURDEN.

IN JUST ONE DAY, AN ENTIRE CITY GOT ERASED, LEAVING ALL OF ITS CITIZENS WITH NOWHERE TO GO. AND TO MAKE MATTERS WORSE, THE ECHOES OF TODAY'S EVENTS HAD SPREAD WITHOUT LIMIT.

SOCIAL MEDIA POSTS AND NEWS STORIES ABOUT THE SO-CALLED "VANISHING MAN" OFFERED PEOPLE A SMALL RAFT OF HOPE AMIDST AN OCEAN OF CHAOS. BUT MOSTLY EVERYONE ELSE WAS STILL IN MOURNING... HAVING BELIEVED THAT DAVE PERISHED IN THE END.

HIS FIGHT WITH TEMBRIS WAS CAPTURED ON FEEDS FROM SECURITY CAMERAS, SO THE FOOTAGE HAD BEEN CIRCULATING ONLINE. I GUESS THE LAST CAMERA GOT DESTROYED BY DEBRIS, SINCE THE VIDEO ENDS JUST BEFORE MY SAVE. WHAT A RELIEF.

HOWEVER, AMIDST EVERYTHING THAT HAD HAPPENED, I WAS SURPRISED THAT DAVE AND I HADN'T BEEN BLAMED FOR OUR ROLE IN CAUSING THIS DISASTER. THOUGH, I'M SURE SUCH A THING IS ONLY A MATTER OF TIME.

IT WASN'T EXACTLY HOW WE PLANNED FOR THINGS TO GO...

BUT THE WORLD WAS CHANGING. JUST NOT LIKE HOW WE THOUGHT IT WOULD.

BUT AFTER ALL, IT IS STILL EARLY IN THE GAME.

AND IN MY OPINION, THERE'S JUST NO SENSE IN GIVING UP UNTIL THAT FINAL BELL RINGS.

BAD THINGS HAPPEN. LIFE'S NOT ALWAYS FAIR, AND SOMETIMES THINGS JUST DON'T GO YOUR WAY...

GET OVER IT. SMILE. AND BE THANKFUL FOR WHAT'S AHEAD.

AFTER ALL, IT'S ONLY AT OUR LOWEST POINT WHEN WE CAN REALLY LOOK FORWARD TO THE CLIMB.

A WISE FRIEND ONCE TOLD ME... "LIFE'S AN ADVENTURE TRAVELED ONE STEP AT A TIME. TAKE A HOP, SKIP, OR A JUMP, AND YOU JUST MIGHT MISS SOMETHIN'.

TAKE IN EVERY MOMENT WITH BOTH EYES AND HEART OPEN. THEY'LL GUIDE YOU TOWARDS SOMEPLACE..."

219

YOU WERE ALWAYS MEANT TO BE.

CHAPTER 7, END. BOOK I, END.

ADVENTURER'S NOTES #7

LIKE I SAID BEFORE, ALPHAGLYPHS ARE
SYMBOLS THAT AN ANCIENT WRITING SYSTEM
CONSISTS OF. THEY ARE KNOWN TO BE ALIEN
IN ORIGIN, AND ARE BELIEVED TO BE DERIVED
FROM THE NATIVE LANGUAGE OF THE MYTHOI.
COINCIDENTALLY, THEY'RE PICTOGRAPHIC,
JUST LIKE MANY OF THE EARLY WRITING
SYSTEMS THAT WE KNOW HAVE
ORIGINATED HERE ON EARTH.

WHAT THIS MEANS IS THAT
THEY'RE MADE UP OF PICTURES, DRAWN
TO LOOK LIKE THE THE OBJECT OR CONCEPT
THAT THEY'RE SUPPOSED TO REPRESENT.
HOWEVER, I'LL ADMIT THAT THEY SORT OF
JUST LOOK LIKE RANDOM DOODLES MADE
BY SOME CRAZY PERSON WHO HAD WAY
TOO MUCH TIME ON THEIR HANDS. BUT
THEN AGAIN, THE SAME CAN BE SAID ABOUT
EVERY WRITTEN LANGUAGE, SO MAYBE I'M
JUST OVERTHINKING THINGS. AND DESPITE
MY INABILITY TO PROPERLY TRANSLATE
THEM, I'VE ALWAYS FOUND ALPHAGLYPHS
TO BE EXTREMELY FASCINATING, IN
THEIR OWN MYSTERIOUS WAY.

SIMILARLY TO MYTHOI RELICS AND
OTHER ARTIFACTS, YOU CAN EXPECT TO
FIND ALPHAGLYPHS IN R.O.O.T. SITES FAIRLY
OFTEN. BUT IF YOU'RE LUCKY, YOU MAY
ALSO SPOT THEM IN MANY OTHER PARTS
OF THIS WORLD... AND PERHAPS
EVEN A FEW OTHERS.

THANK YOU!

THANK YOU SO MUCH FOR READING AEON FORCE!
THIS WAS THE FIRST BOOK I HAD THE PRIVELEGE
OF CREATING, AND I HOPE THAT YOU ENJOYED
READING IT AS MUCH AS I DID WORKING ON IT.
THOUGH THIS IS ONLY BOOK 1 OF A SERIES I PLAN
TO CONTINUE BUILDING OVER TIME, I HOPE THAT
IT WAS A MEMORABLE INTRODUCTION INTO AN
EVEN GREATER STORY, ALTOGETHER. STILL, IF
IT TURNS OUT THAT YOU REALLY LIKED BOOK 1,
BE SURE TO RECOMMEND IT TO OTHERS. A
GOOD STORY'S ALWAYS A WHOLE LOT BETTER
WHEN YOU FIND FRIENDS TO TALK ABOUT IT WITH,
SO GET OUT THERE AND SPREAD THE WORD!
IF THERE'S ONE THING I'VE LEARNED WHILE
WORKING ON AEON FORCE SO FAR, IT'S THAT
IT REALLY IS ALL ABOUT ENJOYING THE JOURNEY!
AEON FORCE IS A JOURNEY THAT WE'RE ALL IN
TOGETHER, SO I HOPE YOU STICK AROUND TO SEE
WHERE IT'LL TAKE US ALONG THE WAY. SPEAKING OF
WHICH, THE JOURNEY WILL CONTINUE IN BOOK 2!
SO, BE ON THE LOOKOUT FOR NEW FACES AND
ADVENTURES WE'LL ENCOUNTER IN THE FUTURE.
UNTIL THEN, KEEP YOUR HEAD UP HIGH AND
CONTINUE SAYING "NO" TO THE IMPOSSIBLE!
WE'LL MEET AGAIN SOON. AND ONCE AGAIN...
THANK YOU!

ABOUT THE AUTHOR

HEY EVERYONE! IT'S ME, THE AUTHOR. YOU KNOW, THE GUY WHOSE NAME'S ON THE FRONT COVER OF THIS THING? YEAH, THAT GUY. TO BE HONEST, I'M A REALLY MODEST PERSON WHO'S NEVER BEEN VERY GOOD AT TALKING ABOUT HIMSELF, BUT I THOUGHT I SHOULD SHARE A BIT OF INSIDER INFORMATION FOR THOSE WHO ARE INTERESTED, SO HERE GOES. EVER SINCE I WAS LITTLE, I'VE ALWAYS ENJOYED DOING TWO THINGS: DRAWING AND TELLING STORIES. GROWING UP, I WAS FORTUNATE TO HAVE BEEN SURROUNDED BY MANY INCREDIBLE BOOKS AND TV SHOWS THAT I COULD ALWAYS TURN TO FOR INSPIRATION. FROM AN EARLY AGE, I KNEW THAT I WANTED TO CONTRIBUTE TO THE GROWING WORLD OF FICTION SOMEDAY. I JUST DIDN'T KNOW WHERE TO START. BUT THEN, IN A SUDDEN MOMENT OF TRIUMPHANT DISCOVERY... I REALIZED THAT NOBODY EVER TRULY KNOWS WHERE TO START. SO, I LOOKED AROUND THE ROOM AND SAID TO MYSELF, "WELP, I MIGHT AS WELL START HERE."

I BEGAN WRITING AND ILLUSTRATING AEON FORCE AS A COLLEGE STUDENT. I SPENT LATE NIGHTS AND ANY EXTRA TIME THAT I HAD IN BETWEEN ASSIGNMENTS WORKING ON THE STORY. ALL IN ALL, IT WAS A HUMBLE BEGINNING, AND ONE THAT I'M REALLY PROUD OF WHEN I STOP AND LOOK BACK ON IT. ASIDE FROM ALL OF THAT, I'VE GOT A BUNCH OF OTHER HOBBIES AND INTERESTS THAT I MIGHT AS WELL TELL YOU ABOUT. IT MAY ALREADY BE SORT OF OBVIOUS AT THIS POINT, BUT I'M A HUGE NERD FOR SCIENCE AND HISTORY (BOTH FACT AND FICTION ALIKE). I'VE ALWAYS BEEN A FAN OF MOVIES, TV SHOWS, AND VIDEOGAMES THAT BRING THOSE TWO SUBJECTS TOGETHER. ADDITIONALLY, I CONSIDER MYSELF A BIT OF AN OUTDOORSMAN WHO LOVES NATURE, EXERCISE, AND WALKING MY DOGS WHENEVER THEY'RE UP FOR IT. BUT WHAT CAN I SAY? I'M A SIMPLE GUY, SO IT'S THE SIMPLE THINGS IN LIFE THAT REALLY MAKE ME HAPPY. AND OH YEAH, ONE MORE THING. I ALMOST FORGOT...

BONUS FACT! MY WORKSPACE IS ALWAYS A CHAOTIC MESS!

I'VE BEEN TOLD THAT A PERSON'S MOST CREATIVE WORKS ARE OFTEN BORN FROM CHAOS, AND I'M TEMPTED TO AGREE. BUT HEY, WHAT THE HECK DO I KNOW? AFTER ALL, YOU'RE THE JUDGE OF THAT.

Made in the USA
Middletown, DE
25 February 2022

61797213R00126